In the Time of Paul

How Christianity Entered Into and Modified Life in the Roman Empire : : :

BY

Rev. Edward G. Selden, D.D

Pastor of the Madison Avenue Reformed Church, Albany, N. Y.

Chicago   New York   Toronto
Fleming H. Revell Company
Publishers of Evangelical Literature

Copyright 1900
By Fleming H. Revell Company

This scarce antiquarian book is included in our special *Legacy Reprint Series*. In the interest of creating a more extensive selection of rare historical book reprints, we have chosen to reproduce this title even though it may possibly have occasional imperfections such as missing and blurred pages, missing text, poor pictures, markings, dark backgrounds and other reproduction issues beyond our control. Because this work is culturally important, we have made it available as a part of our commitment to protecting, preserving and promoting the world's literature.

INTRODUCTION.

THIS little book attempts to set forth some of the more significant facts pertaining to the Gentile world into which the Apostle Paul carried the Gospel of Christ. It is not possible to make an exact division of the composite life of his times and to trace out in all their detail the political, social, moral, religious, and intellectual phases of the old civilization which it was the task of Christianity to recast. The various departments of influence overlap and intermingle; yet in order to set forth the complex conditions with which the new religion had to deal, and out of which it achieved unparalleled results, it seems best to present a series of pictures, outlining in swift succession the special aspects of the world into which Christianity was forcing its triumphant way.

TABLE OF CONTENTS.

Chap.		Page
I.	Paul and His Times	13
II.	The Task Assumed by Christianity	26
III.	The Political Structure of the Roman World	43
IV.	The Social Life of the First Century	61
V.	The Religious Condition of the Age	81
VI.	The Moral Standards of the Period	100
VII.	The Intellectual Tendencies of the Time	122
VIII.	The Inevitable Conflict and Victory	143

CHAPTER I.

St. Paul and His Times

THE Apostle Paul is the representative man of the first century. In him are embodied the moral qualities and the missionary motives by which Christianity conquered the world. It would be unjust to ignore the devotion and service of his fellow laborers. John was of even finer mold. Peter was equally earnest, Barnabas as conscientious; but none embodied so much of power and grace, so much of promise and prophecy. In no other was manifested such persistent zeal and such adroit application of the forces at command. "He was one of the creative geniuses whose policy marks out a line on which history has to move for generations afterward." Not only is this our conclusion upon reviewing the events of the first century, but it must even have been patent to his own clear judgment. By preaching, and by the organization of gathering forces, he felt himself under constraint at any cost to insure the establishment of Christianity in the Empire.

In The Time of Paul

In answering the summons to leadership in the new movement he rose to the sublimest heights of thought and purpose. His very consciousness was transfused by the glory of the undertaking. Partly by virtue of his own energy and partly by force of circumstance he was pushed to the front. He was content to build on no man's foundation, to preach no gospel save that which had been revealed to him, to determine his action by no man's advice, to gauge his fervor by no other man's devotion. He was absorbed in his apostolic mission. Hence came services second in moral quality and effectiveness to those of no other man since time began. Moses was a leader and lawgiver whose labors for his own nation cannot be overrated; David laid the foundations of a kingdom, and gathered the soul of all lands and ages into the music of his psalms; Cyrus appeared as the providential deliverer of a people who could not fulfil their destiny in captivity and exile; Alexander has been ranked by a modern historian next to the Man of Galilee as a promoter of civilization; to the generalship and statesmanship of Cæsar is to be attributed the territorial expansion of the Roman Empire; yet the work of none of these was so absolutely and incontrovertibly vital to the higher interests of

St. Paul and His Times

mankind as was that of the Apostle to the Gentiles. He wrought largely in the Great Western Empire, through which all that was best in the earlier civilizations was transmitted to modern nations. His labors entered into the persistent and progressive life of the ages.

One secret of Paul's remarkable success is found in the nearly perfect combination of hereditary qualities and prerogatives which he possessed. In him mingled two streams of tendency which flowed out of the Jewish and Roman worlds. On one side were ancestry and training, on the other the proud consciousness and the political privileges of a citizen of the Empire. His family had very likely resided in Tarsus long enough to have become identified with its social life and endowed with all the rights and sentiments of citizenship. The Seleucid kings in founding the place had shown a preference for Jewish colonists, so that political favors may have been granted, a generation or two before Paul's time, for distinguished services. While, therefore, the training of youth and the later education of young manhoood in the school of Gamaliel had given him intimate acquaintance with the literature, laws and traditions of his people, so that Jewish feelings were in him peculiarly intense, yet having been born so far from Jerusalem, in a Roman colony and in the midst of Roman influences, he must have had a broader acquaintance with the world and a more catholic sympathy with man than was possible to the other apostles. He appreciated the glory of Jewish tradition and its narrowness, the corruption of Rome and its actual power. In a practical way also he used the twofold advantage of Hebrew birth and Roman citizenship. In every city he went, first of all, where a Gentile would not have been admitted, namely, into a synagogue. He was at home in the simple customs of worship and speech of his people. He could begin every appeal to them on the ground of common faith and hope in the God of Israel, and in his teaching could move along the lines of their Messianic promises to the actual life and teachings of Jesus. To be sure, he met with bitter opposition and cruel treatment, and yet in every town through him as a Heaven-sent ambassador, Christ came to some of His own who were ready to receive Him. This accounts for speedy success in Asia Minor and in Macedonia, in Corinth and in Rome. The Jewish people were already widely scattered. Josephus mentions that by one edict a century before Christ, two thousand families were transported to the fortified towns of Lydia and

Phrygia, for the sake of hastening submission and good order among a rude people. The special political privileges granted by the Seleucid kings to secure the contentment and fidelity of these exiles were confirmed by Roman officials. A people instructed in religious truth was thus established in the midst of heathen communities and in due time a specially prepared Apostle was sent forth to take advantage of their intelligence and influence in disseminating among them the principles of the Christian faith.

At the same time, in many an emergency the protection assured by the universal rights of Roman citizenship secured to Paul life and liberty for prolonged service. At Thessalonica he was kindly received by the Politarchs; at Corinth he was rescued from the hands of infuriated Jews by the justice of Gallio; in Jerusalem he was saved from the excited mob by the interference of Lysias, the captain of the guard; at Cæsarea he was sheltered from the plots of the Great Council by Festus, the Roman Governor; and yet again he saved himself from the malignity of the Jews by his formal appeal to the right of trial at Rome.

Paul represents the aggressive side of Christianity. Zeal for the kingdom marks his whole career, from his divine call to his last impassioned appeal. There were no passive hours for one who had taken up the burden of the world's redemption. The scope of his labors cannot, indeed, be easily understood now that Asia Minor and Macedonia are so remote from the track of modern progress, so far apart from all arenas of national strife. It is difficult to realize how populous was this region at this time. The great highways of commerce and travel lay along its coast, through cities prosperous in trade, magnificent in architecture, the centers of Greek culture and influence; or over the mountain passes of the interior through fortified towns in which order was maintained by Roman magistrates and centurions. Through all of these provinces Paul went with the freedom assured to a citizen of the Empire, and with ever deepening comprehension of the exigencies and opportunities which confronted him.

The story of Paul's providential call has in it a touch of romance.

One day while waiting at Tarsus in doubt as to his future, he suddenly found himself face to face with Barnabas, who, years before, with an instinctive recognition of his zeal and capacity for service, had befriended him at Jerusalem. It was on the crowded streets of this Cilician city that Paul again encountered

St. Paul and His Times

the man who had been praying for a coadjutor in his apostolic labors. Barnabas' word of invitation and appeal was as spark to tinder. The voice of this zealous worker was to Paul like the voice of God, and forthwith the two friends traveled together to Antioch the Syrian capital, where for a whole year they labored together, and had the joy of seeing vast numbers of Gentiles brought into the new covenant.

Here in the third city in population, wealth, and commercial importance in the Roman Empire it first began to dawn on the Roman mind that a religion was making its way which could no longer be identified with the ancient Jewish faith. "The disciples were called Christians first in Antioch," but the inventors of this new name little dreamed that a name so lightly given, at first perhaps with ribald wit, was to penetrate, overmaster and finally outlive by uncounted centuries the mighty empire whose seat of government was upon the seven hills of Rome.

It is significant that this Gentile city, and not Jerusalem, was the starting point for the first great world-wide missionary enterprise; that here began the work which was to extend through every province of the known world. By the light of history it is now easy to see that the very genius of Christianity as

In The Time of Paul

a world-wide religion was in the impulse which sent Paul and Barnabas forth from, and brought them back to, a city belonging not to the Jewish but to the Roman world. It was not so far distant from Jerusalem—the earlier base of religion, where James presided over the first Christian church and where some of the twelve still lingered—as to prevent attendance at the Great Council which was held for solemn consideration of the new and startling enterprise upon which these enthusiastic apostles had entered. The new missionary centre of Christianity lost nothing from being within a few days' journey of the sacred city, while it gained much from its relation to the great world which the Jew called Gentiledom. It was the destiny of the new religion to conquer the all-conquering Empire, in order that the salvation of the world might be achieved through the co-operative agency a people not bigoted and shut out from vital touch with the nations, but cosmopolitan and in active communication with the world on every side of its manifold activities. By reason of its commerce, and of its avenues of communication on sea and land, Antioch was "the Gate of the East," while by its political affinities it belonged to the Western world. No city was so favorably situated with reference to the prosecution of a missionary enterprise which was not to stop short of the Pillars of Hercules and the shores of Britain. Here, where for several centuries had dwelt the Greek kings of Syria, and where at this time resided Roman governors and high officials, was born the undertaking which the centuries have not yet brought to completion.

The pamphlet written by Paul's companion, Luke, under the title of "The Acts of the Apostles," and the occasional letters of the Apostle himself which have survived the vicissitudes of the centuries, give sufficient data concerning his missionary journeys throughout the Empire, and his enforced residence at Rome. It seems probable that a favorable termination of the first imprisonment gave Paul five years or more of continued labors in Asia Minor and Macedonia. This was the universal belief of the ancient church, and is supported by fragmentary utterances of early writers. His disciple Clement, afterwards Bishop of Rome, expressly asserts that Paul preached the gospel "in the East and the West," and that he instructed "the whole world in righteousness." Eusebius, Chrysostom, and Jerome held it as a matter of common knowledge that Paul went into Spain, and this in all probability carried him through Southern Gaul. When at last his life-purpose

In The Time of Paul

had been fulfilled he found a not unwelcome release through martyrdom. He had written of himself as "Paul the Aged," worn out by unnumbered toils and unrecounted sufferings, and more than "ready to be offered." It was a pathetic and yet not inglorious ending of his earthly life. He had tasted the bitterness of loneliness, for he wrote to Timothy: "When I was first heard in my defense no man stood by me, but all forsook me. Nevertheless, the Lord stood by me and strengthened my heart." With this comfort, ineffable and unfailing, he still was able by the very exigencies of his fateful trials to "proclaim the Glad Tidings," in full measure, "so that all the Gentiles might hear the Word." Thus "the tribunal of Nero faded from his sight and the vista was closed by the vision of the judgment seat of Christ." The lights and shadows continued to the end, and he marched to his martyrdom leading captivity captive. In the sight of men it was an hour when evil exulted, and when disaster fell upon the worthy. But he was not forgotten of the Master whom he had served. The angel who had appeared to him in the hour of peril on the storm-tossed sea, "standing by him" in the night, and speaking sweet words of assurance, came again as under the convoy of heavenly attendants he joined "the glorious company of apostles, the goodly fellowship of the prophets, the noble army of martyrs," by whom he would not be counted among the least of the saints of God.

The times of Paul are to the highest degree significant because they gather up the influences of Greece and Rome during centuries of brilliant development, and at the same time cover the period of the decadence of the old philosophy and religion. It was the "fulness of time" for the culmination of divine plans, because never were need and opportunity greater than during this critical period. That a religion so radically different from any phase of thought or mode of worship previously known should have secured a hearing and gained a footing within the empire must be reckoned among the wonders of the world How this came about,—the attempt, the hindrances, the helps, the victories,—is not only a matter of historical interest, but is a source of enlightenment concerning the most essential features of Christianity. Peculiar problems are being constantly faced by missionary enterprises. Now it is the caste system of India; now the exclusiveness of China; the nationalism of Japan; or the stolid baseness of the South-Sea islanders. But at no time did so large and complex a problem present itself as in the middle of the first century. It was a practical question to be solved upon the broadest and deepest principle, and supported by grace and power above any standards then known to the world. Under the leadership of such men as Paul the gigantic enterprise was carried through. Christianity, having sprung out of Judaism, was transplanted and made to flourish alike in the soil of classic and barbarous nations. The new Gospel was proclaimed, the new worship set up, the new order of life established,—and no one can comprehend the meaning and worth of the new religion who does not mark the conditions with which Paul had to deal and the ends which he sought to accomplish. We must understand the task assumed by Christianity in its length, breadth and complexity; the hindrances which were encountered; the unavoidable delays and accommodations; the adaptations and adjustments which had to be made; the many-sided truth which had to be presented to men of many minds; and the crude beginnings of organizations and institutions which had to receive more perfect development. For the initiation of this movement looking towards the evangelization of the world Paul was the "chosen vessel" of God. He was appointed "to go far hence unto the

St. Paul and His Times

Gentiles," as an apostle whose quenchless enthusiasm was to suffice for the most arduous service and whose appeals were to shake the throne of the Cæsars. Born during the reign of the mighty Augustus, he lived through the shameless administrations of Tiberius, Caligula, and Claudius, suffering martyrdom under Nero the fifth emperor and the most depraved. His lifetime, therefore, covers the period of critical conflict between two opposing civilizations. The contest itself belongs to many centuries, but during the ministry of the apostle the mastery of human thought and action passed from Cæsar to Christ. When Paul died Christianity had proved itself a vital force; and to him, more than to any other, belongs the supreme honor of successful leadership in a world-wide enterprise for a true religion and a ceaselessly progressive civilization.

CHAPTER II.

The Task Assumed by Christianity

A RELIGION is to be judged not merely, perhaps not primarily, by what it actually accomplishes, but by what it aims to do. The religions of Greece and Rome attempted little of practical moment. The idea of affecting government, molding society, or even influencing public sentiment by religion was as remote from the classic mind as from that of the mystical worshipers of the East. Mohammedanism began a crusade against an infidel world and from the days of the Hegira sought to win the support of blindly devoted adherents. It has proved itself a mighty force in many nations, and has more than once changed the history of populous lands; but it has not aimed to infuse into society the ideals of gentleness, kindness, nobility and spirituality, and has not succeeded in a dozen centuries in establishing anywhere on the globe a progressive civilization. The Hebrew religion produced a sacred literature which has not yet been outgrown; but with a moral code of superior

The Task Assumed by Christianity

quality, with a monotheism of exalted type, with a history full of promises and pledges of divine favor, it never dreamed of becoming an aggressive and redemptive force among the nations. It was always self-centered. In no epoch of Jewish history did the loftiest of kings and prophets seek to extend the faith or overthrow the idolatrous and abominable superstitions of less favored peoples. Even when unlooked for opportunities presented themselves in Gentile cities like Antioch and Corinth for effective propogandism, the representatives of the Jewish religion were content to build splendid synagogues under the shadow of heathen temples and exult in the exclusive privileges of the children of Abraham. Unlike all other religions, Christianity had its orign in the sublime self-sacrifice of One who came into the world on a mission of love; went about doing good; was lifted up upon a cross that He might draw all men unto Himself; and left the scene of His labors with words of command upon His lips which placed His disciples under an unrepealable obligation to evangelize all nations in His name.

The genius of the new religion was first manifested in the matchless kindness of the Master and then in the re-embodiment of that kindness in His followers. It required some

In The Time of Paul

weeks of meditation and prayer in that upper room where the Eleven had met the Risen Lord, for men who had lived in the narrowness and exclusiveness of the earlier religion to gain understanding, courage, and impulse for so vast an enterprise as the conquering of the world by the Gospel of salvation. But as leaven works in the lump so the Spirit of Christ wrought in them. It was only a question of time when they should be completely leavened.

Having once come into vital contact with One who lived and died for men they could not be long content in the selfish and unproductive enjoyment of a saving faith, whose action terminated in themselves.

Some practical outworking of Christianity seems quite a matter of course to those who have been nurtured in its precepts, and yet was it not a most amazing thing that a handful of obscure men should have assaulted the customs and superstitions of ages with no other weapon than the spoken word; that men who were so provincial as never to have crossed the boundaries of Galilee and Judea should dream of invading the great Roman world with a message from a crucified peasant? Yet that is exactly what Peter and John, and a little later Barnabas and Paul, did. The enterprise upon which they embarked did not seem to

The Task Assumed by Christianity

them desperate, for they had consciously found the distinctive truth of Christianity touching the grace of God and the salvation of men; they also cherished the pledge of companionship and power from the Risen Christ, and longed to replace wretchedness and despair with a peace and joy which should fill the whole world.

The divine origin of Christianity, and its fitness to be the universal religion, are no less clearly demonstrated in its boldness and comprehensiveness than in the benevolence of its attitude and purpose toward mankind. It asserted its right to dominate the thoughts and lives of men, and control human actions with an absoluteness which makes the despotism of the Cæsars seem trivial, and the superstitions of the ancients as passing fancies. For all time it sought to forbid things that once were exalted, subdue passions which once were rampant, demand services which before were unasked; in a word, it sought to bring every thought and imagination into captivity to the obedience of Christ. It is not conceivable that any human mind could have chanced upon so novel a scheme, or that any human heart could have dared such impossibilities. It remained for the unfolding counsels of God to bring into the light a secret hidden from the foundation of the world, to-wit, that the Gentiles were fellow-heirs with the people of Israel, and that by the grace and truth of the Gospel the world itself was to be rescued from moral ruin, and the whole structure of human society rebuilt upon the foundation of a pure faith and an exalted righteousness.

How comprehensive was the work upon which Christianity entered appears from a more detailed study of its stupendous sweep. In the first place, it sought to refine and elevate man; to lift each individual to a higher plane of existence and activity. "You hath He quickened," wrote Paul in appeal to the consciousness of new life and power. Christians are "new creatures" in Christ, of whom great things might reasonably be expected. All the faculties of man were to be aroused and brought into full play by the revelations of the Gospel and the touch of the Spirit. The mind, heart, conscience, and will were all to be regenerated by the Divine message. But the scope of Christianity was never to be limited by the narrow bounds of individual existence. Its aim was the re-construction of society, and it might almost be said that the individual was regarded as a means to that end—the saving of the world. The whole composite life of mankind was to be redeemed and exalted. The whole order of human life was to be radically

The Task Assumed by Christianity

changed, the very atmosphere of the world was to be purified aud vitalized.

To begin with, the sentiments which had prevailed regarding both God and man were to be essentially modified. The frivolity and baseness which characterized Athens and Rome alike grew out of the prevailing notions as to the manner of life which existed among the gods of Olympus and the low standards of character among men. No inspirations came from above and no aspirations from below. No need was more imperative than a revelation of the actual glory of God and the potential glory of man. Here was the splendid opportunity to which the Hebrew people had been indifferent. Their earliest Scriptures contain a sublime portraiture of a holy and majestic God, a gracious and compassionate Jehovah, but they never attempted to displace the Greek and Roman divinities, never thought to drive out the gods of the heathen. The apostolic preaching, however, began with the fundamental truths that God made the world, that He rules in righteousness, that He redeems in love that He wants the confidence and obedience of men who cry, "Abba, Father" and know themselves as sons of God.

Where other religions had been indifferent or easily tolerant Christianity was insistent and

In The Time of Paul

exacting. The uncompromising attitude of the Apostles excited bitter resentment. Alike by their conviction of absolute truth and by their demand for reverence they stirred the skeptical to animosity. Sometimes their heathen auditors mocked, as on Mars Hill; sometimes they persecuted, as in Iconium and Lystra. But no species of opposition prevailed against the determination to create new impressions concerning the dignity of God and the worth of man. Newness of life, a change as deep as the human soul and wide as the human race, could not come while men laughed at their gods and imitated their reputed vices. They must be made to feel the reality of the holy God who made and fills the universe, His nearness to man, His watchfulness and solicitude, His fatherly patience and His helpful grace. They must learn to exact of themselves purity, sincerity, kindness, spirituality, and begin to live together as rational and moral beings upon whom rested the highest sanctions of religion. New ideas and nobler ideals must have currency and insensibly impress upon men the nobility and sacredness of life, the whole of life with its wide range of thought, speech, action and relationships.

This means that Christianity not only sought to introduce a new type of personal character

The Task Assumed by Christianity

but to bring about new relationships among men, and to rebuild the whole fabric of society. The vastness of the undertaking is better appreciated after a study of the social and political conditions of the first century. It is always difficult to rescue an individual from low ideals and corrupting habits, but to reverse the ideas and sentiments of a community, to seriously modify the customs, check the tendencies, and transform the spirit of the world is an undertaking so delicate, so intricate and so complex as to appall the boldest mind. But Christianity could not fulfill its mission until it had entered with regenerating power into every department of the corporate life of mankind, until it had purified and elevated the family, society, government; until it had overcome apathy and dullness, pride and prejudice, passion and cruelty; until it had neutralized the selfishness and worldliness so dominant and so persistent at every grade of life; and until it had so reconciled men to each other as to make harmony and mutual helpfulness the law of their being.

This is the idealism of the Gospels and the Epistles. This is the standard set by the example and teaching of Christ and by the urgent preaching and impassioned letters of the Apostles. If carried out to perfection it

In The Time of Paul

would have amounted to a social revolution, for scarcely any sentiment or enterprise of the heathen world, whether classic or barbarian, approached the new standard. Whatever was unjust or unclean was bound to give way, whatever was of superstition and idolatry was bound to yield to new and higher demands. All Ephesus was in an uproar because, as their opposers admitted, the missionaries of the Gospel had turned things upside down in the great city as they had done everywhere else in Asia. The new evangel which they proclaimed interfered with the profitableness of trade in the silver images of the great goddess Diana, now hopelessly discredited by apostolic preaching. It also took away the cruel gains which heartless men were making out of the wandering fancies and mystic words of a hapless maid whom Paul afterward brought to a sane mind at Philippi. Somewhat later it emptied the Roman temples throughout the Roman provinces and, as Pliny's letters show, turned the stream of industry and trade into other channels than those which had been fed by the crowds of superstitious pilgrims that flocked to the shrines of the gods.

It was in part because Christianity had this high mission that the masterful mind of Paul planned for so many campaigns in the great cities of the empire. If the new order of social life could be established in populous districts, and could illustrate its advantages in great centers like Antioch and Ephesus, Corinth and Rome, a new standard would be set up throughout the Empire. The policy devised and strictly pursued by the Apostle kept him in the midst of the most intense social life of his day, not merely because greater numbers were thus made accessible to his preaching, but also because greatest moral gains were made by counteracting the ancient tides of selfishness and corruption by the wholesome tendencies and kindly impulses flowing from the character and doctrines of Christ. In every city Paul urged such precepts and principles as are found to-day scattered through his Apostolic letters. Men were called to remember that they shared the common life of society and were really members one of another. They were not to indulge in falsehood and trickery, for that would be unneighborly; they were not to steal from one another or seek to corrupt another, for that would be unbrotherly. They were bound by the law of Christ to build each other up in all wholesome and desirable ways. Masters were to be forbearing and patient, servants obedient and faithful; parents were to be

In The Time of Paul

watchful for the true nurture of their children, and children in turn were to give honor and obedience; husbands were to show affection and respect, and wives were to regard the highest interests of the home; in short every relationship by which the members of society are held together and work together was to be sanctified by the spirit of Christ. Under all seeming differences of endowment and functions one spirit was to prevail for the sake of the peace and harmony, the prosperity and happidess, of the whole. One was to use his gift of prophecy, another his property, another his high office, for the good of others. All were to show love with sincerity and mercy with cheerfulness. In every way Christianity was to show itself to be not merely a religion, not merely a form and mode of worship, but a scheme of life and action. It was designed to enter with practical precepts and abounding grace the most sacred domain of the soul and the most complex relationship of society. It was to promulgate a perfect code of morals and at the same time prove itself a social force for the regeneration of human life, for the effective assertion of the brotherhood of mankind, and the realization of the highest social order.

While inculcating an ideal standard of

The Task Assumed by Christianity

thought and conduct Christianity accommodated itself to existing conditions. It was not so transcendental as to lose touch with the actual life of society. It did not refuse its name or its benediction to those who did not fully live up to its sublime principles. For instance, the invariable exaction is that of the Sermon on the Mount,—"Be ye perfect even as your Heavenly Father is perfect." One who has a lower aim is unworthy to call himself a follower of Christ. One who could rest contented while faults of character were apparent would miss the consciousness of likeness to the Master. At the same time there was a patient forbearing with manifest defects and even open transgression when men were sincerely striving to gain the mastery of self and the world. When all of the Twelve forsook their Lord in the hour of darkness and panic when the mob broke into their retreat in the olive garden on the slope of Olivet he had no word of rebuke. An hour later their leader was denying his friend and master in the palace of the High Priest! Yet the Risen Lord sent a special message of love and confidence to Peter, and came again and again to the Upper Room for tender conference with the Eleven. Paul wrote the seventh chapter of his Epistle to the Romans in frank exposure of his pitiful struggles against the passions and tendencies of the flesh,—but he also penned the eighth chapter in which he rejoices that condemnation no longer rests upon him, but that he is living in the Spirit, and that he has the witness of highest authority, namely that of his own consciousness, to his Sonship with God.

With the same recognition of the necessarily imperfect stages of social life Christianity adapted itself to prevailing laws and customs. Its ideal never fell by the breadth of a hair below absolute reverence to God, loyalty to justice, and love to man; and yet from the first it bore patiently with the established order of things, waiting for the time when its precepts would banish cruelty and lust and inaugurate the reign of peace and prosperity. Christ said, "Render to Cæsar the things that are Cæsar's," that is, the things that are his not by the "divine right" of kings, but by the order of established government. There was never a Cæsar who sympathized with the teachings or accepted the demands of Christ—not even Augustus or Marcus Aurelius; but often, as in the case of Tiberius and Nero, they violated every instinct of humanity as well as every doctrine of pure religion. Yet Christ let the injunction stand unqualified—"Render to Cæsar the things that belong to him." Paul

The Task Assumed by Christianity

learned from the teaching of the Master the duty of reverence for constituted authority, and joined with Peter in urging obedience and loyalty to "the powers that be." Some legalized form of government is a practical necessity. Nothing is more perilous than anarchy. Even heathen magistrates are set for the repression of crime. They insure the continuance of society.

Not that Christianity was never indifferent to injustice or tolerant of imperfection. It held inviolate the principles of manhood and brotherhood. It never abated by a single jot or tittle its imperative demand for sincerity, fairness, gentleness and kindly service. While, therefore, it temporarily accepted the law and administration of the Roman Empire it was fundamentally at variance with the corruptions and oppressions incidental to such a godless exercise of political power. It was not the form of government to which the new religion opposed its tenets. The political order might be imperial or democratic, the headship of the state might be determined by heredity or election, but every ruler was under obligation to govern in the fear of the Lord and in the interest of humanity. Christianity was fearless of consequences, while unflinchingly maintaining its moral standards.

In The Time of Paul

Proclaiming principles of kindness and justness it went boldly forth to take its chances of life in the great heathen world.

It is important to emphasize the fact that that it is the mission of Christianity to cover the whole human life with "religious sanctions." It stands apart from nothing that pertains to thought or action. Every department of human existence furnishes a field for "applied Christianity." In the words of Paul, "Whatsoever you do, do all to the glory of God," we have an injunction which is both extensive and intensive. There is no hour of life when the obligation does not press upon men to love God with all their heart, and their neighbor as themselves. There is not a project to be cherished nor a fancy indulged in which springs from a loveless spirit. There is not a relationship in private life nor a function in public administration that is beyond the law of love and a good conscience. To interfere as little as possible with the common, everyday life of the citizen has been declared to be the ideal of government; but it is the glory of Christianity, and its unique distinction, that it has to do with every detail of life. It assumes the herculean task of controlling all the affairs of the world, in the interest of the highest manhood and of the perfection of social

The Task Assumed by Christianity

life. The king on the throne is not above the level of its exactions, the slave is not beneath its benison. The solitary wanderer is sought by its messengers. The crowded quarters of the world's capital are illumined by its truth and made tolerable by its grace.

The demands of the new religion were inexorable, yet it went everywhere on errands of mercy and love. Into a dark, spiritless, hopeless world it made its way with a message of cheer. In contrast with the "fanatical mysticism" of the oriental religions, the "gloomy faith' of the old Etruscans and Druids, the nerveless mythologies of the Greeks, and even the bigoted exclusiveness of Judaism, Christianity was charged with hope and help for all mankind. It had no esoteric doctrines; no hidden mysteries which were for the initiated few. With open page or voice it proclaimed to the multitude the redemption of the world and the birthright of all believers. Its life was in its message, its power was in the living word.

In the year 70 A. D. Titus declared before a Council of War, at the gates of Jerusalem, that the temple must be destroyed in order that the religion of the Jews and of the Christians, which he identified as one, might be the more completely extirpated. His first mistake was in supposing that either form of religion was detrimental to the interests of mankind, or of the Roman state. His second blunder was in calculating upon the overthrow of Christianity in the destruction of either temple or city. The vital elements in this religion are its noble truth, its revelation of the righteousness and lovingness of God, and of the essential sonship of man. The word having once been spoken, after the silence of the ages, the echo could never be lost. The message having once been delivered could never be forgotten. When the covenant which the Lord had made with Israel was annulled, it was not by way of exclusiveness, but of greater inclusiveness. Then was given the wider covenant which would never be retracted;—"I have set thee for a light of the Gentiles, that thou shouldst be for salvation unto the uttermost parts of the earth."

CHAPTER III.

THE POLITICAL STRUCTURE OF THE ROMAN WORLD

IT is not in the least derogatory to Christianity to say that in its attempt to dominate the world it depended upon outward circumstances; yea, upon the rarest possible combination of outward circumstances. This may seem to make the redemption of mankind rest upon fortuitous conditions; it may seem to identify its mission with historical happenings of most unusual and unlooked for character; yet that is a universal characteristic of the divine plan in every realm of activity. It appears in every critical event in history and in every form of life. Not a plant comes to blossom and fruitage without passing through a thousand vicissitudes; not a project for liberty and prosperity but runs the gauntlet of menacing difficulties and oppositions. Moses attempted the release of his countrymen from the oppressions of the Egyptian government, but was obliged to save himself by a hasty flight and a desert exile of forty years.

In The Time of Paul

There was just one weak Pharaoh to be held in check while a million bondmen marched to freedom through the land of Goshen and across the sea. There was just one Persian ruler broad enough in sympathy for a captive people, and large enough in plans for a far away province, to make it possible for men of Judah to return and rebuild Jerusalem.

The "fulness of time" to which Paul alludes had reference not merely to the intellectual and moral attitude of the Chosen People but also to the conditions prevailing in the Gentile world. The hour had at last come when Christianity would find events favorable to the spread of its doctrines and the organization of its adherents. It would have gone down with the Egyptian dynasties, it would have been overrun and trampled to fragments by the Persian invasion, had it not been upheld for centuries by the strong hand of Rome, until it had become mightier than the Empire itself. It not only found protection, under the ægis of Rome, but it came into vital touch with all the elements of ancient civilization which had been conserved, and with the beginnings of a new civilization which was destined to supplant the old. One of the profoundest and most sympathetic of modern historians has said that "Rome is the bridge

Political Structure of the Roman World

which unites while it separates the ancient and the modern world." To take advantage of the figure, Rome is the bridge on which Christianity crossed from the old world to the new—albeit, it took four or five centuries in crossing. Christianity came into the old world, but it belonged to the new. The old world was to be made new in very large part by its implanted truth and infused energy. From the first it had to do with the whole of human life, individual and social, religious and political. Therefore it was concerned with the institutions, laws and customs, the arts and letters, of all peoples. Ulhorn has said: "The ancient world culminated in Rome, and Roman history is the rise of the Empire." Yet culminating as it surely did in such a natural expansion as the world has never seen, it was near to declining. At the opportune moment came the uprising of a new and saving religion. All that was valuable, in fact, all that was salvable in the civilization of antiquity was swept within the lines of the advancing armies of Rome. There it was found by Christianity, and by the time of its transference to the fostering care of new and independent states abundant opportunities had been afforded for the application of the principles and forces of the new religion.

In The Time of Paul

Melito, one of the early Apologists, emphasizes the fact that that Christianity and the Roman Empire were born at the same time, with providential adjustment to each other. It is a proverb that the significance of historical events cannot be adequately appreciated by those who are near the field of action; but the relations between the religion which proclaimed its mission to redeem the world, and the political power which had mastered the world, was patent to philosophical observers of that very age. Indeed, this relationship did not escape the writers of the earliest literature of the new religion, though they could not have anticipated, of course, the illuminating records of the great centuries which were to follow.

Luke wrote as simply as we date our correspondence: "Now it came to pass in these days, there went out a decree from Cæsar Augustus that all the world should be enrolled"—thus locating in current history the year when Joseph and Mary went up from Galilee to the City of David. It was a matter of interest to fix the time of the birth of Jesus Christ, but the significant thing about it is that it should have been done through its connection with political events.

The birth of Christ is not said to have happened so many years "since the building of Memphis" or the "capture of Babylon," or even the "rebuilding of Jerusalem," but in the very year in which *Augustus* issued a certain edict. Christianity dated its birth by that of the Empire, and now every empire dates its documents by the birth of Christ.

One cannot read the history of Christianity apart from that of the Empire, from the reign of the young Augustus to the day when the senate gave over the government into the hands of the Germanic Odoacer. Wherever Roman organization had gone there went Paul, the wise and masterful leader of the religious movement for the conquest of the world's conqueror. The relations between the two empires, religious and political, were those of rivals. On the whole, however, the emperors furthered the interests of Christianity, although not seldom they were bitterly hostile. We have, therefore, to recognize the combination of unfavorable with favorable influences coming out of the tremendous and widely extended political sway of the Empire. At times its whole force was arrayed in uncompromising opposition to Christianity, history recording no fewer than "Ten Great Persecutions." This was inevitable. In the nature of the case a rapacious political power

In The Time of Paul

could not tolerate the pretensions, to say nothing about the actual gains, of the new world-religion. It was a comparatively easy matter to adopt a new national or tribal deity—a few local divinities, more or less, being a matter of smallest concern. They were all of the same order and could be fused into the common life. They might even contribute something to the state by deepening the loyalty of some new people of the ever widening empire. The state would even have taken Christianity under its protection and patronage if it would only have made a few concessions to the ancient faiths and the supremacy of the government; but that was, of course, impossible. It would have been an abrogation of its most distinctive claim. Early ignorance regarding the unique features of Christianity did secure temporary exemption from harsh treatment. For some decades it was fortunately classified with the prevailing religions. But when it began to manifest its absolute and exacting monotheism; when it began to reveal its purpose to modify the whole life of man; when, above all, its tremendous claims began to justify themselves in the numbers and the devotion of its adherents, then was aroused first the suspicion and later on the animosity of the Roman officials. Even

Political Structure of the Roman World

during the life of Paul hostilities broke out. The great City of Rome was profoundly stirred against the new faith, and Nero became the first of a long list of persecuting emperors.

Yet although the new faith came into such irrepressible conflict with ancient beliefs, and crossed swords with the armed representatives of the government, it could not have conceivably conquered the world except for the Empire. It won its way to lasting victories by virtue of the aid unwittingly furnished by a political power which suddenly changed the tolerance of days to the hatred and persecution of centuries. For hundreds of years Christianity had no successful mission beyond the boundaries of the Roman Empire, and to this day, save on a continent then undreamed of, it has no vigorous and independent life except in lands which at the end of the first century were under the subjection of the Roman legions. This fact adds significance to the geographical extension of Roman authority. The Empire became at last unwieldy and fell to pieces by the weight of its far-away provinces, but the genius for organization and administration, for compelling order and unity, was so gigantic that for a long time it held conquered districts as component parts of the great whole, although widely separated by distance and by national characteristics. The Roman eagles were known all the way from the Atlantic to the Euphrates, a distance of three thousand miles, which relatively is far greater than to-day is the circuit of the globe. Upon another line of measurement the legions marched from the African desert and the Cataracts of the Nile on the South, to the Danube and Rhine on the North, and even to the firths of Scotland, enclosing within their outer lines probably not less than a hundred million diverse people. Not many familiar names greet one who turns to a map setting forth the Empire at the time of its greatest extent; but if we were to designate the countries as they are known to the world at the end of the nineteenth century there would be included nearly all the states of modern Europe except Germany and Russia; all of north Africa, then populous and flourishing; all of the Turkish Empire, then composed of some of the richest and most civilized of Roman colonies; all of Armenia and Mesopotamia, from the Caspian Sea to the Persian Gulf.

An immense service was rendered to Christianity, as the universal religion of mankind, by bringing this congeries of peoples into substantial unity. It was, to be sure, first of all an enforced unity, and to the end was more formal than real, yet it was sufficient to make the impossible possible. Until they were cemented together under the Cæsars, these nations had lived apart, with the utmost indifference to each other's welfare, or more frequently in mutual antagonism. But nations became provinces and were covered by the one name which was infinitely more powerful than all the independent national titles taken together. The parts were articulated into one body politic. They shared in the dignity and good fortune of a single government. They came to have common ties, common interests, common feelings. They stood together in all that concerns safety and general welfare. There was an exchange of garnered treasures, material, social, and intellectual. The heterogeneous mass of countries and peoples became in many essentials homogeneous, "All the elements of culture and all the forces of civilization being comprised in one empire.'

At any previous time in the world's history since the people were scattered from the plains of Shinar, Christianity—if it had existed—would have been confined within the boundaries of a single country, and compelled, if it depended then as now on natural laws of

In The Time of Paul

development and propagation, to share the fate of the country in which it was planted. Not even the *idea* of a universal religion would have been then conceivable. It was the establishment of the empire that broke down narrow national limits and destroyed walls of social partition. For the first time an aggressive policy, with a sustained missionary activity, became possible.

The unity which gave the long looked for opportunity was of advantage first of all in developing a sentiment of kinship among men. In some measurable degree men came to feel a sense of brotherhood between different nations. Whereas once there had been repulsion now there was attraction acting through the common bond of pride and advantage in the empire. Carthagenians and Romans, Greeks and Parthians, dwellers on the Euphrates and inhabitants on the Nile were at last on friendly terms. Differences of name and speech, of origin and political history, were covered over by the larger fact of likeness and partnership in a government of overwhelming majesty. And this feeling the more readily influenced men because of the universal condition of peace. For a time the war trumpet was silent, swords were beaten into ploughshares, and the doors of the Temple of Janus were closed. As one by one the wars of conquest were ended the work of peaceful administration began, and hostile tribes and belligerent nations were robbed of even the incentives to strife. By the end of the first century Epictetus could write: "Cæsar has procured for us a profound peace. There are neither wars nor battles, nor great robberies, nor piracies."

This favorable exemption from sanguinary struggles which would have disturbed communities and absorbed thought, was followed by the helpful administration of Roman jurisprudence. We are accustomed to magnify the *genius* of this people for law and order, but their proclivity in this direction is not mysterious in its origin. The conditions of social and political life on the bank of the Tiber, in the earliest centuries, were such as to necessitate statutory provisions for the establishment of harmony. With so many clashing tribes and rival classes there was no other *modus vivendi*. The very existence of society demanded clear definition and rigid enforcement of rights. Both the idea and the practical application of law grew with the growth of the city and of the Empire. Within the walls which encircled the Seven Hills the contentions of noble and peasant, of patrician and

In The Time of Paul

plebian, which were transmitted from generation to generation, compelled the Senate to limit privileges or grant them, as the case might be. Outside of the walls the smaller cities and kingdoms were scheming and fighting for grants of land, right of trade, and prerogatives of government.

Hence came about in the insensible progress of centuries, first municipal regulations, then colonial privileges, and after that a provincial system of government which covered the earth with its protecting mantle. It was a superb development of law and order, but its origin and development are not mysterious. No social or political facts are more easily accounted for, but they are not for that reason any the less significant.

How great an advantage came to Christianity from the quietness and security of life even in remote provinces is readily seen. The new religion did not seek to place itself in authority as immediately controling men and money and directing political affairs, like Mohammedanism, for instance. All it claimed was the privilege of undisturbed labor, the opportunity to preach its truths, to form churches, to do its silent, unobtrusive work in the midst of society. It was therefore of the greatest moment that lawlessness should be repressed and outbreaks speedily checked. It is not difficult to understand how Paul could enjoin respect for heathen officers of state. "Put them in mind to be in subjection to rulers, to authorities, to be obedient." "Let every soul be in subjection to the higher powers; the powers that be are ordained of God. For rulers are not a terror to the good work, but to the evil." In every city and village of the Empire were courts and magistrates to administer with Roman dignity and authority laws of justice in regard to property and life. The details of such a widely extended system must have been countless, but they were provided for in the settled and comprehensive policy of Rome. All provinces were alike in the eye of the law, in Italy or Spain, in Macedonia or in Celicia. Some communities were less refined and orderly than others, but there were magistrates for Paul to appeal to, if he would, in the exercise of the right of his Roman citizenship, in Lystra and Derbe, as well as in Caesarea and Philippi.

Next in importance to the firm administration of law, which must be accounted an absolute necessity, was the extension of civilization. The special features of Grecian culture require more careful consideration than can be here accorded them, but the general statement

In The Time of Paul

can safely be made that enough of mental quickening and social refinement went into the provinces along with the armies of occupation to greatly facilitate the progress of the Gospel. This preparatory work was not altogether devoid of noble motive, although no emperor adopted such a definite and vigorous policy as that of the Apostle to the Gentiles. The Roman people were proud of their eminence and believed in their mission to civilize as well as to govern the world. More or less consciously they were instruments of righteousness in developing ideas and institutions among nations which they had lifted out of sheer barbarism. Multitudes who would otherwise have been too dull or base to give intelligent hearing listened responsively to the lofty truths of the Gospel. This was true in the provinces of Asia and equally true in western Europe. For instance, a half dozen years after the beginning of Paul's ministry Claudius came back to Rome from the shores of Britain, where he had gone to complete the conquest which Julius Caesar had begun a century before. When Claudius crossed the channel the island had no readiness for the Gospel. Rude, untrained Britons, to whom words of gentleness and appeals for mercy would have been as empty sounds, roamed the forests. But the Emperor was a herald of better things. He supposed himself to be merely annexing another barbarous province, but he was, in truth, planting the seeds of civilization and opening the way for a more benificent reign than that of Imperial Rome.

The same significant changes were wrought on the other side of the British Channel. A century before Christ, what has become the fair land of "sunny France" was savage in every aspect of human existence. The Commentaries of Cæsar not only recount his victories over Celtic and Germanic races; they also disclose the grade and conditions of life along the streams and among the forests of Gaul. We are made to see the rude huts rising above the river banks, the warriors in savage dress with barbarous weapons grouped in scattered villages, or wandering to and fro in half-aimless migrations. We hear the sound of their clannish warfare and of their baser orgies. As thus we look into the darkness and behold brutish instincts and low ideals we wonder how a message of peace and righteousness could ever reach such minds and influence such hearts. But Cæsar's work for the Romanizing of Gaul bears an intimate relation to Paul's work for the christianizing of the land. The Apostle followed the General a century later,

In The Time of Paul

and the spiritual conquest was the speedier and more complete because of the earlier victories of arms.

Another advantage came to Christianity through the provincial system of Rome. Routes of communication were opened and guarded throughout this vast territory. One rides out of the ancient capital to-day over highways which were in their perfection under the emperors. One enters the City of Chester, the outpost of British occupation, over roadbeds which were laid eighteen hundred years ago; and adventurous explorers have traced the lines of imperial roads over the passes of Phrygian mountains. It was a simple necessity of administration in the provinces. Five main lines of travel came out of the Imperial City and branched in every direction—through southern Gaul into Spain; through France to the Scottish border; through Milan and over the Alps to Cologne and Leyden; through Philippi and on to Ephesus and Antioch. A traveler could measure his way along a circuit of seventeen hundred miles, by Roman milestones, with Roman maps in hand. Along these far-extended routes there was a constant stream of travel for military or commercial purposes, so that no herald of the Gospel need lose his way or be hindered in his journey.

Political Structure of the Roman World

Christianity entered Rome before the eager Apostle could fulfill his desire to proclaim the gospel at the capital of the world. Pilgrims and men of commerce were constantly passing from Palestine to Italy, and not a few bore with them the message of salvation. Some statesmen regarded with disfavor the inflowing tide of immigration from the East, complaining that "the Orontes was pouring its waters into the Tiber;" but if they had been wise and well informed they would have rejoiced that men of a new faith could find their way to Rome, and that swift and faithful Messengers could traverse all lands with parchments which had been illuminated by the hand of one who was a citizen of the Empire and a preacher of righteousness.

Christ delayed His coming until Cæsar had pushed his conquests from the sea to the great rivers, and humbly built His kingdom where an earthly potentate had in some sense laid the foundation. So heaven has often condescended to be helped by the world. But where the earthly king pitiably failed the Heavenly King gloriously succeeded. When the Empire could do no more for the civilization of the world the Kingdom took up the work and carried it on: carried it on moreover not only with divine patience but with

In The Time of Paul

divine assurance; and it will continue to carry it on until the might of Cæsar is surpassed by the gentleness of Christ.

CHAPTER IV.

SOCIAL LIFE OF THE FIRST CENTURY

IT was Christianity's mission to remodel the social life of the world, beginning with that of the Roman Empire. With this in view it entered into existing conditions, and maintained a temperate and flexible adjustment to them. Before it was a problem of incalculable difficulty, for there was very little in the structure of life, either at Rome or in the provinces, which corresponded with the ideals of a pure religion. In the entire round of existence Paul would have searched in vain for any occupation or diversion which had been influenced by sentiments appropriate to Christianity. Neither in private nor in public life would he have encountered the motives and standards which he represented in his own inspiring and devoted life. In the Forum he would have found judges, pleaders, spectators; in the market he would have heard the discordant cries of buyers and sellers; in open courts before the temples he would have witnessed dancing, dice playing, and all sorts

In The Time of Paul

of frivolous amusements; at the public baths he would have listened to idle chatter, gossip, jest, and story; at some of the great domestic establishments he might learn of protracted feasts followed by unspeakable revels, but nowhere would he come into contact with forms of social life which had been elevated and beautified by such ideals as were embodied in the Gospel

What could a preacher and advocate of rightousness do in the midst of activities and relationships so completely out of accord with the standards upon which he must insist? If he was wise he would not demand that individuals should step out of the ranks of society, withdraw from accustomed engagements, and break all ties of kindred and friendship. Christianity aimed to do its regenerative work for the corporate life of mankind as well as for elect individuals. Paul followed the policy adopted by the Divine Master, who was his pattern and leader. Christ began with Peter, Nicodemus, the woman of Samaria, and Zacchæus, undismayed by their crudeness, accepting them as disciples at the earliest stage of development, and even going on to "call" other men and women as worldly as these had been. In pursuance of the same policy he took his place at a feast given by a retired collector of customs, who had invited many publicans to meet him as his friends; and some years later he even asked for hospitality at the hands of such an official at Jericho. Again and again it is recorded of Christ that He was the guest of some Pharisee, whose every notion of life and religion was unlike His own; and, doubtless, if the centurion had shown gratitude for the recovery of his boy by a gathering of Roman officers to welcome the Miracle Worker, he would have courteously met the social demands of the hour.

Later on in the century, when apostles were planting religious truth here and there throughout the Empire, it became necessary, in the same way, to bear with conditions wholly at variance with their standards. An infinite number of perplexities arose in every community, as the Epistles bear evidence; they being largely devoted to practical questions which had been referred to the Apostles for settlement. When Christians could not determine what their religion permitted or required, especially in churches which were part Gentile and part Jewish, in homes half Christian and half heathen, and in occupations and ceremonies wholly unsanctified, they sent a messenger to the Founder of the church to ask how He would apply the principles He had preached, and so help them to readjust their disturbed relationships. The kind of questions He was asked to answer was: Under such and such circumstances what concessions could be safely made; under such and such demands by heathen officials or un-Christian husbands how much could be properly granted?

To study the social structure of the Empire in the first century is to find new ground for admiration for a religion bold enough, gentle enough, delicate enough to adjust itself to such diverse and unfriendly conditions, and yet mighty enough to triumph over habit and passion, over dullness and perversion, and at last modify the long-established order of ancient Rome.

Consideration of the social life of any age should begin with the family, for that has always been and must ever be the basis of society. Among the Jewish people there had resulted from the training of many centuries an ideal of home life immeasurably superior to that of contemporaneous nations. Both tradition and written precept inculcated kindness in parents and obedience in children. Very much was made of the family life. Every analysis of social life came at last to this unit. The nation was divided into tribes, the tribes into families. In each family the father was under bonds to give tender care and training to his child and the "first command with promise" enjoined upon children was the honoring of father and mother. Wherever a synagogue was found the Apostles took swift advantage of the instruction that had already been given in righteousness and kindliness; and the infusion of religious sentiments which in every community came from Jew to Gentile must have greatly facilitated the work of the Gospel. Outside of Israel there was properly speaking no home life. In the early and vigorous days of Rome marriage had been crowned with the highest honor, and for centuries divorce was unknown. But by the time of Augustus the family institution had fallen into shameful discredit and the position of women —which of itself determines the grade and quality of civilization—had become deplorable. There is nothing in the teachings of Christ to correspond with that Grecian thought concerning woman and her place in the family which was adopted at Rome to its incalculable injury. "Plato represents a state as wholly disorganized where wives were on an equality with their husbands." Aristotle expressly characterizes women as "beings of inferior kind."

Family life, in the true meaning of the words,

the Greek did not know. He sought happiness elsewhere than at his own hearth. "Is there a human being," asks Socrates of a friend, "with whom you talk less than with your wife?" Demosthenes acknowledged that philosophy had not enriched the home. It could not, because it was fundamentally at fault in this regard and threw itself directly in the path of a religion in which were strict injunctions for kindness and purity in the closest relationships of life.

It is not to be supposed, however, that the marriage laws had become utterly powerless, and the institution of the family utterly without value. It had once been both the glory and the strength of the nation in the good old days when the Roman matron was respected for her virtue and cherished for her loveliness, and the old marriage laws could not be repealed nor could the sentiments from which they had sprung be entirely uprooted. So far as the provinces were concerned, also, there was a large remnant of power for social purity and good order in the ordinances which were enforced among the rudest peoples. Those only were recognized as having the privileges of Roman citizenship who had been born of legitimate marriage; which was an immense advance upon the indifferent customs of orientals and savages. The influence of the higher type of civilization and of the constant enforcement of law was felt throughout the populous regions of Asia Minor as a check upon the license which had been prevalent, and undoubtedly proved an educating and constraining force toward a higher grade of social morality.

The lowest depths were reached in the great cities, especially in Rome. The reasons for this are not far to seek. All tendencies to evil melt together into a mighty current in a thoroughly godless city, and in the world's capital the stream of lust and worldliness swept everything before it, like a swollen torrent. The sanction of religion was quite absent from the ceremony of marriage, which came to be regarded as merely a civil contract, easily made and easily dissolved. Very often young girls were disposed of, according to the whim or the political or financial advantage of their parents ; in fact, the Latin has no phrase in which a suitor could seek the consent of a maiden to honorable marriage. It was an arrangement between other parties than those most concerned, making noble sentiment and generous purpose absolutely foreign to an ill-assorted union, which frequently brought strangers under a bond which might never be otherwise than distasteful to them.

Marriage took the girl from a life of irksome and profitless seclusion, and in a day bestowed upon her almost boundless liberty, liberty for which she may have longed, but for the proper use of which she had not been trained. She could for the first times sit at feasts, visit freely temple, circus, amphitheater, and even the public baths. It is not to be wondered at that distate for marriage grew into formidable proportions among men. The large majority refused to accept the valueless bond, until patriots like Metellus appealed to men to marry, not for the blessings of companionship and a home, but, with better prospect of cordial hearing, for the sake of the state.

Out of such marriages as these proper home life could not issue. Parents had neither love, nor the sense of responsibility, toward their offspring. The father had absolute right over the disposition of his child and was restrained neither by law nor by public opinion from neglect or cruelty. For the most part, in the degenerate days of the Empire, children were accounted a burden, and were frequently disposed of by exposure. Infanticide became frightfully prevalent. In no case were the

Social Life of the First Century

children who were allowed to live nourished with maternal care, or trained with paternal solicitude. At an early age they were sent to a slave or freedman to be taught the rudimentary principles of reading, writing and arithmetic ; thus often being exposed to the most demoralizing influences. Later, if their education was to be carried on further they began to read standard authors in both Greek and Latin ; such as Homer, Virgil and Horace. The next stage brought them to a rhetorician for discipline in public speaking, which was deemed the high road to "success;" the next to the lectures of certain philosophers. They were also put under the physical training of professional athletes. As to moral teachings we have conflicting reports. Very often it must have found no place in a course determined by an ambitious but dissolute parent; although high-minded men, like Pliny and Quintilian, would doubtless seek to develop reverence for justice, decency and patriotism. In rare instances Roman youths completed their studies by extensive travels through the Empire and by residence at Athens.

The preaching of Paul evidently dwelt largely on the mutual obligations of the home; for emphatic and repeated commands are to be found in all of his Epistles. His words must have

In The Time of Paul

sounded strange to most of his auditors and in many households must have awakened new affections and made real the relationships which had before only a nominal existence.

Society was divided into classes which were differentiated by marked characteristics. In our time, when problems touching the common life of humanity excite profound consideration, it is pitiful to see the divergencies which in every great city rend asunder the mass of population. So was it in Rome. There was as nearly as possible a reversal of ideal conditions. It was not so much a question of "social order" as of social disorder; not so much an enquiry regarding "general prosperity" as the prevalence of universal wretchedness. "The whole structure of pagan civilization was really based on a foundation of crushed and forgotten humanity." The lower orders of society scarcely find mention in the writings of the day. We have at command volumes of history, letters, orations and poems referring to every phase of existence among the favored classes, but there are no pictures from the lives of the lowly. We know enough in a general way about the debasement and squalor at the bottom of society, among the submerged nine-tenths, enough for tears and groans in behalf of the hopelessly wretched, but the details are lost forever. Luxury and pride paint themselves vividly, though in a grotesqueness of which they are unconscious, but groveling poverty does not care to put itself upon canvas. It is only by piecing together scraps of information and inferences gathered here and there that we are able to reconstruct a social condition which becomes more and more remote from prevailing types of civilization.

Christianity suffered unavoidably from the class distinctions and conflicts of the Empire, just as it has been compelled to go halting through India, by reason of the caste system. It was not only hindered by the greed and lust of the rich and by the incapacity and misery of the poor, but its precepts of industry and manliness were nullified by an unyielding contempt among every class for all forms of work.

Labor was not only wanting in honor, it was under the ban of public opinion. It was considered disgraceful to engage in productive enterprises, thus making the existence of a sturdy "middle-class," which has always proven the reliance of progressive nations, absolutely impossible. Even Plato justified the contumely which was heaped upon those "whose employment would not permit them to devote themselves to their friends and the state." Aristotle taught no higher wisdom;

maintaining that "all forms of labor which require physical strength are degrading to a freeman," on the ground that "Nature had created for such purposes a special class." Even the noble minded Cicero is on record as asserting that "the mechanic's occupation is degrading," because "the work-shop is incompatible with anything exalted." Every word and act of the Founder of Christianity, every trait of His character and every impulse of His grace, is opposed to such a rating of men and to the continuance of social separations. Christianity had a message of dignity and hope for all; it asked only for honesty and earnestness in such pursuits as were possible in the ordering of life for each man, but its voice was drowned by the clamor of the "privileged" and the outcries of the wronged.

At the summit of society were the nobles, of hereditary rank, and the wealthy, of whom not a few had climbed from lower levels, from the most part by trickery or truckling. But in comparison with the multitudes they were not numerous. The patricians were never in a majority and were not relatively increased by the influx of population from every province of the Empire. The very rich depended upon enormous grants of land and the unwilling and poorly requited services of the lower

Social Life of the First Century

orders. In Nero's reign half of the province of Africa belonged to six great landlords. Officials amassed incomputable fortunes—millions upon millions of sesterces, but the Senate was a limited corporation, and financial magnates like Pallas and Narcissus are quickly enumerated. From the height of the few we make a long descent to the next lower stratum of society. The absence of the self-respecting middle class,—independent farmers, artisans, traders,—who could feel themselves a part of the corporate body, having free and satisfying industries, and bearing a share of responsibility for the general welfare, precipitates us to the level of men who could endure public disregard and contempt. Even the professions, especially medicine, were in the hands of freedmen and slaves. Architecture, sculpture and painting were considered unworthy occupations for aristocrats. Thus through the unreasonable pride and vanity of the day, many men of intellectual power and artistic genius were barred from wholesome and profitable pursuits, which were degraded by the hands to which they were relegated.

Beneath this class of workers, small in numbers and esteem, came the uncounted mass of men who, in two well defined classes, paupers and slaves, made up the greater part of

In The Time of Paul

the population in the first century. The dependent poor of the great city may be divided into two sections, the majority, who were abject in their poverty, and the minority, who made some pretension to comfort and respectability. These were destitute of property and were only saved from reliance on the daily dole of bread from the hand of the state by private benefactions. It was a part of the vapid sentiment and senseless display of the age that rich men should parade their dependents before the public, a fashion which proved equally ruinous to both parties. The patron in lavish magnificence of dress, was accompanied through the crowded streets by throngs of attendants who performed insignificant or imaginary services and offered every conceivable kind of flattery and attention. There was no manly and productive employment for such poverty-stricken individuals, and consequently they lived in a state of miserable, degrading parasitism. Even men of respectable origin dragged honorable names down to the mire of ignominy, counting it almost a boon of fortune to live in pusillanimous dependence upon the bounty of those men who treated them with almost limitless contempt.

There was, nevertheless, a lower depth of infamy and wretchedness for the common herd

Social Life of the First Century

of humanity, whose hunger was appeased by public largesses of corn, and whose dangerous restlessness was held in check by the diversions and excitements of the amphitheater. Rome was crowded with such irresponsible people who had flocked thither for the very purpose of eating the bread of idleness and worthlessness. It has been estimated that the Capital contained not fewer than two hundred thousand of thèse wretched and debased creatures, who made up the mobs which howled at the public games and wasted the rest of the day in frivolous and demoralizing amusements. The distribution of corn to this dangerous horde was not in the least prompted by charity. It was regarded simply as a measure for the safety of the state. This social residuum was looked upon as a part of the political and social constitution of society, and as beyond mitigation by any measures or motives known to the Roman officials. Even at its best the policy of the emperors only temporized with the evil which grew apace. Every gift and concession tended toward further pauperizing and debasement. The multitudes fell into more absolute and hopeless destitution, and the mobs grew more and more reckless and exorbitant in their clamors for relief and favors. The fear increased lest an out-

In The Time of Paul

break from this accumulated mass of irresponsible humanity should overwhelm the lives and property of the few who had so much at stake.

This fear was enhanced by the possibility of a slave insurrection; for in the social reckoning there were tens of thousands who were more miserable than the paupers, in that they lacked even the semblance of freedom. Beneath every other social level was a mass of slaves, exceeding in number the entire remainder of the population. These were the chattels of the Roman people. They were not even thought of as human beings, but they nevertheless throbbed with the common life, and imperiled society by their degradation and unspeakable wretchedness.

This iniquitous system was not merely entrenched in immemorial custom, but existed, irrational and inhuman as it was, by virtue of the uniform teachings of philosophers and sages. It had the sanction of the highest authorities in ethics. The slave was not a man. There belonged to him neither free will nor claim to justice. Even Plato, "the noblest thinker of antiquity," maintained that slavery was a natural institution. Aristotle taught that the ideal household was provided with two sorts of instruments, inanimate and animate; slaves without souls and slaves with souls; but the soul of a slave was regarded as imperfect because devoid of will. So mightily did such sentiments sway even the best of men that Cicero apologizes for the grief he could not altogether suppress upon the loss of a slave to whom he had become attached. "Sosithenes is dead," he wrote his friend Atticus, "and his death has moved me more than the death of a slave should"—just as to-day, one might be chagrined to be found in tears over the loss of a dog pet. The Roman law made careful distinctions against this hapless portion of humanity. The slave was not a person, but only a thing, and therefore the absolute property of his master. This, of course, made marriage an absurdity, and although there was no escape from the phrases which indicate human relationships the words were declared to have no legal meaning. There were "families" of slaves, with the "father" or "brother," but these terms were as nearly as possible emptied of significance when applied to bondsmen. The slave market was a chattel market. The vendor cried his wares, the buyer examined his goods, the purchaser treated his newly acquired property according to the whim of the moment. During the day slaves worked in chains; at night they were huddled in barracks half under ground. They were branded, flogged,

In The Time of Paul

crucified, according to the pleasure or passion of the owner.

In wealthy households their work might be light and the conditions of existence less rigorous. Indeed, slaves were multiplied, in vulgar display of extravagant luxury, until they became a burden and embarrassment because no sort of employment could be devised for them. Curious offices were invented as a relief to the situation. There was a "folder-of-clothes;" a "custodian of Corinthian vases;" a "sandal-boy," whose sole occupation was putting on and removing his master's shoes; "letter-carriers," and attendants without number. Such slaves made up an idle, unwilling, almost unmanageable household, under direction of a head-slave who was responsible for their behavior and industry. Besides these, there were a few educated slaves: secretaries, librarians, and readers, who, on the one hand, ministered to the pride and self-indulgence of their masters, and on the other, scarcely felt the instincts of manhood or womanhood. The whole system was hopelessly enervating and debasing.

To study the social structure of the Roman Empire is to discover the gigantic task assumed by Christianity in its unique undertaking to uplift the entire life of mankind. To elevate the consciousness of the individual, to purify and enoble the home, to adjust the various classes of society to harmonious relations and wholesome industries, to cover the whole existence of man with the sanction of a pure and exalted religion, this was the enterprise upon which Christianity went forth into the world. It endeavored not merely to bring about social order but to infuse something of zest and dignity into the occupations of life; to make men conscious of better things than those which in the round of an idle, luxurious life brought only weariness and despair.

> "On that hard Pagan world disgust
>   And secret loathing fell;
> Deep weariness and sated lust
>   Made human life a hell.
>
> In his cool hall, with haggard eyes,
>   The Roman noble lay:
> He drove abroad, in furious guise,
>   Along the Appian way:
>
> He made a feast, drank fierce and fast,
>   And crown'd his hair with flowers—
> No easier nor no quicker pass'd
>   The impracticable hours."

Only the word which Paul as a messenger of Him who came to make all things new carried to Antioch, Ephesus and Rome, a word of authority, of inspiration, of hope, a word for manliness, kindliness and humanity, could so

In The Time of Paul

check the tendencies and remold the social life of the age as to save the world from self-disgust and self-destruction.

CHAPTER V.

THE RELIGIOUS CONDITION OF THE AGE

RELIGION had in the earlier centuries of Roman life no small influence on the character and conduct of the people. The seriousness which characterized the senate was determined by a universal and sincere belief in the presence and favor of the gods; and the marriage vow gained its sanctity from the worship of the Lares and Penates. It has occurred among most peoples that the early stages of religion have been free from formalism and grossness. Out of the stress of primitive life, or out of the genius or inspiration of select individuals ideas and forms of worship have developed rapidly, only to lose their vitality in a few centuries. Zoroaster undoubtedly contributed enough of moral and religious truth—much of which is still preserved in the Zend-Avesta—to reform the Iranian people; working in noble fellowship with the king, as in a yet more favored land Isaiah wrought with Hezekiah, and brought the religious life of the Jewish nation to a

In The Time of Paul

comparatively high standard. His religious system lacked, however, the virility necessary to withstand adverse influences; in the course of centuries falling away from the monotheism and morality which had given it vitality, and losing itself in dualism and image worship. The people had received gleams of light from Ormuzd but the illumination was neither complete nor constant.

Scholars who are conversant with the Vedic Hymns declare that the standard of thought concerning the nature of God and the spiritual life of man is immeasurably above that which appeared among the Hindus in later centuries. The religious fervor spent its force and degeneracy followed.

At Rome adverse influences proved too powerful for a religion which never produced a literature to compare in ethical qualities or in spirituality with that of Persia or India, and which in the time of the Empire had come to exert but small influence upon private character or public life. It had fallen into such decay that no longer were men eager to build temples, altars, and statues to divinities to whom unquestioning worship had once been rendered. This degeneracy may have followed the influx of wealth and luxury, or it may have been the penalty for the despoiling of

The Religious Condition of the Age

Greece. Undoubtedly the Hellenic type of religion had proved destructive of Roman simplicity, in respect alike to faith and morals. The Greeks had a genius for philosophy and art but not for religion or morals. They exactly reversed the traits and tendencies of the Hebrew people, who scarcely commanded the rudiments of philosophy and showed no inventiveness in the realm of beauty, but were in all periods of their national life profoundly alive to the sublime truths of religion; while the Greeks manifested, even in the palmiest days of intellectual greatness, a strange lack of reverence and seriousness.

Rome incorporated a civilization which was in many phases an advance upon her own but failed to exclude its fatal tendencies. It was all very well to admire the delicate play of fancy, so much more free and venturesome than that of the more practical Latins; but it was to the last degree unwise to exchange a sober habit of mind for the frivolousness which had prevented the development of manhood among the Greeks. If the graceful Grecian myths had been built upon a profounder sense of the unity and grandeur of the universe and of human life, the Romans might have adopted and rechristened the personified forces of nature not only without moral deterioration but with quickened and chastened fancy, a process both beautiful and beneficent. Their own traditions were heroic, not religious or poetical. They might have added refinement to strength if they could have assimilated the legends which had grown up in Grecian literature to account for the many fascinating phases of nature, and at the same time have retained their sobriety and virility of character and their strong sense of right and justice. They might then have turned with advantage to look upon Old Neptune as the god of the sea, upon Ceres as the goddess of the harvest, upon Vulcan as the god of fire, or upon Venus as the goddess of beauty. They needed to become more versatile and imaginative but they could ill afford to barter their stern virtues for all the arts and letters, for all the fancies and legends of Greece, together with the light-mindedness and lax morality which disfigured the Peloponesian civilization. The matter-of-fact Latin mind weighed down the airy Hellenic fantasies with a grossness foreign to the original conceptions. The genius of administration and war which characterized the Romans was of a very different order from that which had created and peopled Olympus.

The Religious Condition of the Age

It excites no wonder to learn that the divinities were sometimes publicly and bitterly scouted. It has been said that the whole Olympian family would to-day reside in a penitentiary. Every imaginable crime of lust and rapacity had, in the degeneracy and prostitution of fancy, been attributed to the gods; not even Jupiter, the father of all the gods and the noblest, escaping the imputation of jealousy and chicanery. Long before the Roman conquest the Grecian code of morals had become corrupt, and the common standards of life had become subject to vanity and passion; thus reproducing the order of things exemplified by their deities. Rome absorbed the evil with the good, and the decay of her own religion was swift and pronounced. First of all, it lost its grip upon the most intellectual classes, because they were the earliest to detect the baseness of motive inseparable from current legends, and were the most fearless and independent in action. Later on it relaxed its hold upon the masses.

The day had passed when Pericles led the procession with songs and flowers, up to the heights of the Parthenon; and when the generals of the republic brought their thank-offerings for victory to Capitoline Jupiter.

In The Time of Paul

The day of unquestioning reverence and faith was irrecoverably gone.

Here and there devout souls, retaining their mystic fervor, came as of yore to the temples as sincere petitioners. Some of the noblest and purest, like Tacitus and Plutarch, refused to yield up their serious belief in the gods and renounce their respect for the national religion; but the indications are abundant and convincing that the power custom formed the larger factor in the observances of the time. The great Cæsar made bold to announce his scepticism. Lucretius indulged in bitter and sarcastic allusions to religion, while Pliny coolly assumed that the assured result of science was to banish all gods from the universe. Cicero said that hardly could an old woman be found who trembled at fables about the infernal region. Juvenal declared that even the boys scoffed at the idea of a world of spirits. Cato wondered how one augur could meet another without laughing in his face. The universal accompaniment of such scepticism was as usual a childish and tyranizing superstition, an absurd and grotesque simulacrum of faith.

While Cæsar presented himself before the public as a scoffer at religious beliefs he never entered a carriage without uttering a magical

The Religious Condition of the Age

formula. Augustus, who at banquets had made merry with the gods, dreaded misfortune all the day when he had put a shoe on the wrong foot. Pliny, a self-proclaimed atheist, wore talismans. When a bird of evil omen sat on the Temple of Jupiter all the people were summoned to make solemn expiation to avert disaster from the state. Superstition was almost universal, and everywhere potent. An earthquake shook the hearts of men, an eclipse shut out all the light of heaven, a flight of birds brought terror to the stoutest souls, and a serpent crossing his path dismayed the boldest warrior.

In the year 37 of the Christian era an earthquake shattered the splendid city of Antioch to its foundation. It had boasted of being the Athens of the Orient, and justified its claim to intellectual distinction by its galaxy of wits, philosophers, rhetoricians, poets, and satirists. Yet under the terror of that awful hour all the citizens became the easy prey of a mountebank whose name has been preserved through the centuries. He professed to be able to turn aside the portentous horrors by talismans of the most ludicrous description, and the wisest became the unworthy dupes of his magical arts. It was a time for necromancers and astrologers to reap their harvests.

In The Time of Paul

Nevertheless, something of religion outlived both scepticism and superstition, and manifested itself in punctillious and exacting observances. These religious acts were not of great moral value; but some lingering of religious sentiment, some sense of dependence on supermundane powers, some flickerings of heavenly light must have sustained a system which was subject to open and deserved contempt. In a way, though not the highest and noblest, the state had been founded on religion, and even in the degenerate days of the Empire men could not utterly ignore the faith of their fathers nor suppress their own instinctive aspirations. Plutarch, in that very century, dared to write: "Sooner may a city exist without houses and grounds than a state without faith in gods. This is the bond of union and the support of all legislation." At every important public transaction the gods were consulted and sacred rites observed. No senator at Rome under Augustus could take his place without going to the altar of his diety and there offering libations and strewing incense; and every city and village throughout the provinces had special rites for its protecting divinity.

In domestic life the religious exactions were no less rigorous. Every important event

The Religious Condition of the Age

in the family was celebrated with religious services. The goddess Lucina watched over the birth of a child; Rumina attended its nursing; Nudina was invoked when on the ninth day the name was given; to Statina was consecrated the day on which the child first stepped on the ground; while Cunina constantly averted the evil enchantments which threatened its life.

Rome was excessively punctillious in things religious, the perfection of religion being thought to consist in exactness of ritual. If the substance was gone there was no lack of outward forms. On every ship that sailed out of the harbor at Ostia stood the image of Neptune, and as it passed beyond his vision the merchant prayed to Mercury for success in all his commercial enterprises. Before the harvest a sacrifice was offered to Ceres for a bountiful crop. The ancient temples still stood in their wonted magnificence and were daily visited by multitudes. Feasts and sacrifices were celebrated with pomp, and altars were the resort of suppliants for divine favors. Even emperors performed solemn rites in behalf of the city's welfare. Whatever may have been the extent and sincerity of disbelief among the intelligent classes it was still necessary to support popular standing by open adherence to the religion of the state.

Then as now women in greater numbers than men gave time to religious observances. It may indeed have been largely due to the wives and mothers that the customs of worship were so long retained in the home. Cicero might ridicule some of the stories told about the gods, but he nevertheless deemed it a desirable thing, a thing to be taken as a matter of course, that his wife should cultivate piety. Plautus gives an interesting portrait of the ideal wife. Among such womanly virtues as dignity, respect for parents, and obedience to the husband, he does not fail to name reverence for the gods. What Paul found at Athens he might have discovered at Rome or Ephesus. The people made a display of religion. The paraphernalia of worship was not wanting. "The old world was full of gods." It was said in humorous exaggeration by a satirical observer of the age: "Our country is so peopled with dieties that it is easier to find a god at Athens than a man." Life was touched at every point by the forms and rites of religion, and if there had been intelligence and genuineness the state would have been saved from the corruptions which were undermining it; but all the faiths which had been

The Religious Condition of the Age

adopted by Rome with such indiscriminate haste and lavish hospitality had alike become hollow. They were all void of life and power. They were all equally impotent. The individual and the state were alike left undefended against moral evil, and uninspired to the noblest ends of life.

In the first place they failed to uplift and purify daily life. They were external rather than internal, formal rather than real, emotional rather than ethical, being utterly devoid of influence upon either reason or conscience. They were not constructed upon this basis. They made no attempt to be effective in the realm of conduct and relationship, they made no appeal whatever to the motives or sentiments of the worshiper, they modified in no conceivable degree his views of life or his methods of securing pleasure or profit. A Roman came to the altar with an offering or libation hoping thereby to discharge his debt to the gods, that they might bear him no ill will, or that they might prosper his enterprise. He recognized a certain obligation to the divinities as the very word which he used for religion implied; but his "religion" did not bind him to a Being august in righteousness and stern in demands of purity. The gods whom he sought to placate were themselves

In The Time of Paul

fickle and lustful, and were, by their reputed character, the last objects in the universe to stimulate men to honesty, highmindedness, and self-control. They had been conceived and created, by the unsanctified fancies of men, and were decidedly materialistic and worldly, even although they were assigned to the mystic heights of Olympus, above the clouds of heaven.

The Greek found beauty in his religion and sought to cultivate in connection with temple and image his æsthetic sensibilities, but he never dreamed of holiness in connection with the Celestial City and the palace of Zeus. A solemn procession in which the sacred robe of Pallas was carried up the heights of the Acropolis and within the gates of the Parthenon had no imaginable relation to manhood and womanhood. The attendants of all ages and both sexes pressed forward with oil and cake for the sacrifices, but without the slightest enthusiasm for righteousness or kindly service. They could not fail to be impressed by the majestic proportions of the temple which crowned the summit, nor to delight in the noble pediment which the genius of Phidias had fitly adorned, but they neither saw nor heard anything to enhance the solemnity of life, or to restrain from frivolity or self-indul-

The Religious Condition of the Age

gence. Such psalms as in the days of Pericles were being sung in Jerusalem were as far beyond the comprehension of the cultivated Greek as of the nomadic wanderer in the Lybian desert. It would have been worth all their masterpieces of art to have listened but once to a choir of Levites chanting:—

"Who shall ascend unto the hill of the Lord?
And who shall stand in his holy place?
He that hath clean hands and a pure heart:
Who hath not lifted up his soul unto vanity,
Nor sworn deceitfully,"

or to have found on some scroll the outcry of a penitent soul:

"Search me, O God, and know my heart; try me and know my thoughts; and see if there be any wicked way in me, and lead me in the way everlasting."

The religion of the Greeks never produced a hymn in praise of truth and chastity, nor an inspiration after nobleness and usefulness. Much less did the plagiarized Sacred Songs of the Romans. Lacking the aesthetic sense of the people they had conquered they lost that touch of grace and charm which came to Athenians with their artistic forms. With their own degeneracy they attributed all degrees of cruelty licentiousness to their deities until their religion was not only uninspiring

In The Time of Paul

but often positively corrupting. More than one moralist under the Empire sought to divert the people from the dissolute fancies engendered by current legends of the gods of Rome. Seneca cried out in disgust and despair that: "All shame on account of sin must be taken from men before they could believe in such divinities."

As all the imported religions failed to inspire lives of piety, virtue, and gentleness, so they failed to satisfy the instinctive yearnings of men for comfort and peace of mind. Men are never so imbruted as to become incapable of tenderness and aspiration. Certainly, out of the thronging millions of the Empire not a few souls had voiceless longings for something which did not come to them in fierce battle, in successful intrigue, in hours of revelry, or even in the temple services. Their deeper natures were stirred but no fountain of comfort was known to them. If some eager missionary from Jerusalem, some far wandering minstrel of Judah, had only come to Athens with a message and a song then Rome might have echoed with hymns of gladness, and hearts that were over-burdened and weary might have exclaimed, "I will lift up mine eyes unto the hills, from whence cometh my help. My help cometh from the Lord which made

The Religious Condition of the Age

heaven and earth. He will not suffer my foot to be moved; he that keepeth me will not slumber." It is pitiful to see how they lived on in empty pleasure or dumb despair, never finding what they most needed. Plato, indeed, protests against Atheism as an impossibility, because man cannot banish from his heart, however brave his words of denial, an instinctive belief in the gods. But in the gods of the Grecian and Roman world, there was little to comfort one who blindly reached forth his hands toward the host of Olympus! There came to greet him no assurances of a personal creator and friend, no pledges of watch-care and fellowship, no promises of blessedness either here or hereafter. Of this world of beauty and sunshine, of passion and pleasure, it behooved him to make the most, for beyond it lay the regions of Hades, an underworld, dark, mysterious, uncanny, where incorporal shades wandered aimlessly and hopelessly. Against the weariness, disappointment, shame and disgust of life Pagan religion set absolutely nothing of cheer or comfort.

As these religions of Rome failed to comfort the heart so they failed lamentably to satisfy the mind. While there had been a decadence of religious fervor and a loss of ethical impulse there had been a gain of intelligence. The

In The Time of Paul

habit of investigation and of philosophical speculation had become more general and controlling. Consequently, the myths and fables which had satisfied the minds of an earlier and cruder age and even furnished something of inspiration to character, fell short of the demands made by a less imaginative but more reflective people. Instead of becoming more simple the legends of the gods became more complex and diversified until they broke down by the weight of their own accretions. At last they were too gross and too conflicting to hold even the most credulous. There was, besides, an unmistakable drift toward monotheism, due not only to intellectual progress, but also to the necessities of a moral and religious feeling which began to make itself felt in spite of the corruption of the time. Jupiter still mingled in human affairs and displayed pitiable weaknesses; and yet he, as the father of gods and men, kept on flashing the lightning from the clouds and governing by his sovereign will. The thought of supremacy and unity probably gained more in real than apparent influence on the thought of the age. It certainly acted powerfully on the minds of the thinkers who were pioneers for the people in realms of philosophy. The whole fabric of heathen religion, with its myths, auguries, and libations, trem-

The Religious Condition of the Age

bled before the scrutiny to which at last it was subjected. Once brought into the light of rational enquiry its puerilities, absurdities, and inconsistencies were manifest. Many a legend was punctured by historical study, and many a childish story discredited by a closer acquaintance with the forces and laws of the physical world. Even the wisest did not hit upon a satisfactory explanation of the origin and meaning of life, but they discovered enough to make them sceptical concerning the ancient faith, and irreverent toward the ancient gods.

In their relation to Christianity the religious experiences of the first century were significant in a twofold way.

First, they make pathetic and appalling exhibition of men's need of a religion which should hold within it enough truth to meet every intellectual demand, enough of tenderness and sympathy to satisfy the deepest yearnings of the human heart, and enough of moral excellence to uplift and purify the life of the individual, the family, and the state. Men existed for naught and labored to weariness with no profit because they were given no ideals of manhood, because no appeals were made to their better nature. There was a crying need of a religion which could address itself to the conscience; which could awaken a consciousness of the divinity above and within men; which could present objects and aims large enough and noble enough to make life worth living; and stigmatize with infamy the cruelties, frivolities, and lustful abominations which characterized the society of the period.

There was not only a conscious need but also an unconscious readiness for Christianity. The preparation was not of the positive sort furnished in the sacred writings of the Jews, by their sublime portraiture of a just and merciful God, by their treasured promises of deliverance and ever deepening desire for the coming of the Lord's Anointed. The preparedness came from the exhaustion of all human resources and the hopeless discrediting of the national divinities, set against the irrepressible hopes and yearnings of people who could not quite suppress the aspirations of heaven-made souls.

Though Rome gave such cordial welcome to all national divinities and acquiesced in sacred rites of every imaginable form, still she did not find the religion for which she waited with conscious and unconscious need; and so the processes of scepticism and neglect went steadily on. A state of chaos unparalleled in history took the place of the old national religion out of which in due time a new world was created. The one world-religion of all history made its appeal to that which is deepest and most ineradicable in man; in order that where all other religions had hopelessly failed it might find an open field for beneficent and triumphant work. What the unordained forerunners of the Apostle brought to Rome in such stories as travellers and merchants could tell about the Man of Galilee, Paul finally proclaimed by written and spoken word. Thus was introduced into the Capital of the world a religion which was fitted to supply the needs of the world and at last to accomplish its regeneration; a religion in which should be manifest more and more the wisdom and power of God; a religion which should alike answer man's longing for a life of substantial worth and dignity and for assurance concerning a yet nobler career beyond the tomb; a religion which was to meet with rebuffs, be for a time feared and hated as arrogant and exclusive, but which nevertheless was to prevail against misunderstanding and designing hostility until in the end it should be crowned by a Roman Emperor as the religion of the State.

CHAPTER VI.

THE MORAL STANDARDS OF THE PERIOD

THE difficulties which confronted Christianity in the first century were radically different from those encountered by a founder of the Mosaic system. Out of their centuries of degradation under the Pharaohs a nation of bondmen brought dullness of mind and corruption of morals, but there was no attempt to mold them at once to the divine pattern of thought and life. The legislation upon which was to be built a new order of social and religious life was merely kept in advance of actual attainment, and had often to accommodate itself to hopeless weaknesses and perversions.

Christianity was much more than a code of laws. Its high office was not to legislate, but to instruct and inspire. Its mission was to give to the world a standard of thought and motive which could never be surpassed or outgrown. The amazing thing, therefore, is that it was able to gain a footing in so corrupt an age and maintain its influence in the face of

The Moral Standards of the Period

such base notions and debasing customs as those which obtained throughout the Roman Empire.

It was impossible to accomplish more during the first century than to organize scattered churches, made up of crude and inconsistent Christians, and to proclaim principles which were left to win their way to favor by their inherent excellence. The glory of the "Apostolic Age" has dazzled the modern church until men look back despairingly to it as to a golden period for the return of which we must hope in vain. True it is that the personal devotion of Paul and the spirituality of John are still unsurpassed, and beyond question the heroism of Christian martyrs, even in the earliest centuries, puts to shame the self-considerateness and cowardice which in some degree characterize many modern disciples; yet it must not be overlooked that the cause of righteousness was in desperate straits during the time of Saint Paul and that by only the smallest margin it won its way against the persistent forces of evil which had held sway for generations.

The doctrines of the Nazarene were too novel and too advanced for the majority of the Emperor's subjects fully to comprehend them at first, much less to accept and exemplify them. The crudest notions of life and the basest customs prevailed, and even within the covenant of the church made themselves shamefully manifest. The apostolic letters are the unwitting memorials of a condition of things which no longer survives save in startling exceptions to the rule of decency and correctness of living. Then it was not an unheard of thing for an apostle to reprove a church for drunkenness and unseemly strife at the holy communion, or to warn against such transgressions as blasphemy, perjury and adultery. That men and women, who had been moved by the preaching of the gospel to undertake lives of godliness, should be guilty of such wide departure from the standards of the Sermon on the Mount was made possible only by long established habit, and by the absence of public sentiment against such enormities.

It is happily difficult, if not impossible, for the average Christian to reproduce even in imagination the order of moral life which characterized the Roman Empire. Nor need it find place even in our fancy save in its general features and for the sake of an intelligent appreciation of the task successfully undertaken by our religion. Christianity was indeed as a light shining in a dark place. As a candle in a deep, dark mine, as a diamond in a muck

The Moral Standards of the Period

heap, as a lily among thorns, so was the sweet Gospel of Christ in the great world of the Cæsars; a message of faith, hope, and love, of forgiveness, aspiration, and holy endeavor among men of inherited and acquired viciousness. Farrar has declared that "the epoch which witnessed the early growth of Christianity was an epoch of which the horror and degradation have rarely been equalled and never exceeded in the annals of mankind." It was a time of sad decadence for a civilization which had manifested earlier glories of aspiration and achievement, and which had created two splendid types of national development, but which had spent its vital forces and demonstrated its fatal weakness.

Uhlhorn holds it incontrovertible that "the heathen world was ethically as well as religiously at the point of dissolution," that "it had become as bankrupt in morals as in faith, with no power at hand from which a restoration could proceed." Seneca said of his own times, "All things are full of iniquity and vice, more crimes are committed than can be remedied by force. A monstrous contest of wickedness is carried on. Daily the lust of sin increases, daily the sense of shame diminishes." Juvenal, Tacitus and Pliny are not less severe in characterizing the immoral aspects of the age. Petronius cries out in despair, "Rome is like a field outside of a plague-stricken city, in which you can see nothing but carcasses and the crows which feed upon them."

There were no redeeming features, no hopeful aspects, among any class, from the meanest slave to the monarch on the throne. There was nothing to inspire hope in the regeneration of human society, or respect for life itself. Of the four weaklings who assumed the reins of government after the death of Augustus, and who thus in turn became the most influential men in society, not a commendatory word has ever been spoken. Tiberius was a sanguinary tyrant who came to weariness of life and self-detestation by reason of senseless excesses; Gaius was an unrestrained lunatic; Claudius was an "uxorious imbecile," and Nero a conceited monster and heartless buffoon—of whom a historian has written that he represented " the omnipotence of evil in the apotheosis of self." The habitual intrigue, the acts of murder, the indulgence of outrageous passion which made themselves at home in the palace of the Cæsars, also domesticated themselves among the people. For once wickedness was suffered to run riot that a picture of its grotesque horrors and revolting ugliness might be painted for all time, to

The Moral Standards of the Period

show "the exceeding sinfulness of sin" and the absolute demand for the redemptive work of a Power that can make for righteousness. When cruelty, lust and treachery have done their worst there remains nothing of hope,—save in a moral re-birth of the world.

To analyze the ethical characteristics and tendencies of this age is to make profound study of a ruinous experiment, which manifested itself in an attempt to build a great civilization upon a basis of unsound morals.

To begin with, there was everywhere a fatal lack of seriousness. Strenuousness of life was unknown. The existence of men and women was aimless and valueless. Life throughout the Empire was of the type which depressed the great Apostle when he wandered about the streets of the most cultivated city of the ancient world, and which is parenthetically described in the words: "Now all of the Athenians and the strangers sojourning there had leisure for nothing else than either to tell or to hear some new thing." The most innocent of all their occupations, and the one which commanded their most serious attention, was the rehearsal of the latest bit of gossip. In contrast with the gravity of the old Roman was the trick of levity which had been caught from light-minded Greeks. Their art and philosophy were meritorious but utterly unproductive of earnest living. They could not make out the secret of such a man as Paul. He was indeed a curiosity at the capital of Achaia. They looked into his deeply marked face, suffused with sad reflections as he wandered under the palms, or made his way among the chattering throngs of the market place. When he spoke it was with the speech of a man charged with a portentous message, but they had only listless wonder as to what this "babbler" would say, for he seemed, indeed, to be a "setter forth of strange gods."

There was no sense of reality in such living. It was all a mockery and pretense, and men scarcely took themselves seriously. When Augustus, who gives his name to this brilliant period, came to his death bed he asked a friend "whether he had fitly gone through the play of life,"—as if all the world were in very truth a stage and all the men and women merely players who took the parts assigned them, and who at the close begged the applause due to those who had finished their roles to the satisfaction of idle spectators. Not even into literature and oratory could anything of sincerity and down-rightness be put by men whose temper had been cast in the mold of Roman civilization. Rhetoric and oratory

The Moral Standards of the Period

were the fashion of the hour, and they were studied not for the sake of gaining power to express noble thoughts and enforcing appeals for justice, but merely for the employment of high sounding words and the use of graceful gesture. In all the art of the day there was nothing but studied affectation and elaborate sophistry.

The cause of such universal hollowness and frivolity is not far to seek. There was an utter lack of religious sanction for human life. Their gods were as idle and purposeless as the people themselves. There came from the heights of Olympus no illumination and no voice of stern command; and hence even the religious philosophy of the time was either powerless or perverting. Stoicism had much to say about deity but without the faintest hint of personality. It spoke of the "Reason" of the universe and of an ' Organizer," but this shadowy divinity was identified with law and substance, and sometimes even with the soul, which being in some sense corporeal was at death to be re-absorbed into its Creator. Such a philosophy can only with the utmost stretch of courtesy be called "religion," for it touches very lightly the spirit of man and imparts no impulse to duty or or to manful service. Epicurianism was yet further from inspiration to

In The Time of Paul

nobleness. Atheistic and materialistic, the followers of this easy going philosophy scoffed at the notions which hinted of a Creator, a moral government, or a life for man beyond the grave. They looked upon soul as like the body, save that it may have been made of finer atoms, and they believed that it would be dissolved when the visible part fell into decay. Even its instinctive cries were drowned in laughter as the cup went round and boon companions took up the refrain: "Let us eat and drink, for tomorrow we die."

After all, man cannot live without some absorbing aim, and failing one that is normal and worthy he will turn to what may prove ignoble and worthless. It is, therefore, not surprising that, living for luxury and passion, men so far perverted the chief end of existence as to devote thought and energy to the pampering of the body. They not only became selfish and self indulgent, but inventive and enterprising in providing new forms of pleasure, and in stimulating passion. The Stoic philosophy was nominally but not vigorously and effectively opposed to such devotion to sensuality. Its favorite maxim read, "Do nothing in excess," but it was never enforced with moral earnestness, and consequently offered no resistance to the tide of evil which swept over the nation.

The Moral Standards of the Period

Stoical apathy forbade deep-seated concern even for things which concerned the highest welfare. It made too much of the law of self-preservation, and of equanimity of mind. When philosophers of this school declared that "the essential thing is to live according to nature" they condemned excesses of all kinds, and without doubt many applauded their easy-going theory of life. The precepts of Seneca are admirable: "Pray and live as if the eye of God were upon you." "Live every day as if it were your last." "Live for another as you would live for yourself." "Nature bids me assist *men;* wherever, therefore, there is a man there is room for doing good." But the tenor of Stoicism was against intensity of feeling and discouraged either indignation against corruption or zeal for the regeneration of society.

Luxury was possible only to a small minority of the people. Half of the population of Rome in the first century were under the bonds of slavery while the great mass of free-born inhabitants were only in a lesser degree abject, being beggars, idlers, parasites, the objects of contempt and the victims of cruelty, without hope or aspiration above an existence of squalor, misery and vice. Above these hapless creatures, so far as outward and wordly conditions

In The Time of Paul

are concerned, was an ever diminishing number of wealthy and noble citizens. In external things the upper class were in striking contrasts with the frightful want and groveling habits at the other end of the social scale, but in respect to virtue and temperance they offered few points of superiority. They suffered from ennui and self-disgust; and although hopelessly weary of such a profitless existence they only plunged more deeply into sensuality or devised new forms of so-called pleasure. They had no higher ideal of enjoyment, no other resources of delight. Animalism in more or less refined forms ruled the day. Gastronomy took rank as a science, and gluttony assumed incredible proportions. Delicacies were imported from every quarter of the known world, and banquets, which lasted the night through, became the talk of the time.

The public baths at Rome, the impressive ruins of which have outlived the centuries, came to occupy a prominent place in social life. They were not hygenic but delicately sensual. They were constructed and frequented for enervating luxury, vapid amusement, profitless gossip. Having no serious demands upon their time the wealthy thought it worth their while to build these structures of public resort of

The Moral Standards of the Period

splendid proportions, and to decorate them with imported marbles and gorgeous mosaics, and furnish them with every conceivable device for entertainment. Besides making provision for air and water baths of many varieties, they added gymnasia, lecture halls for poets and rhetoricians, libraries, walks, fountains, and lounging rooms. These new forms of asthetic life which were introduced by Agrippa were worthily developed by Nero and his successors until they became the most popular institutions for the leisure class who were overladened with empty and purposeless hours.

Devotion to luxury was attended with an inordinate love of display. The pride of life took the direction of rivalry in the exhibition of wealth until even philosophers were caught by the craze for meaningless and useless show of expenditure. In order to indulge this passion for display it was necessary, of course, to secure money, and hence came avarice and rapacity. Men were bold and unscrupulous when that served their purpose, and obsequious and sycophantic when servility promised more than insolence. War for plunder and rapine attracted many, while dishonest dealing and violence at home scarcely excited comment. At the same time every man of influence and affluence was attended by

In The Time of Paul

suitors and schemers whose self-debasement had bottomless depths. By the most contemptible means gigantic fortunes were accumulated. Even Seneca, whose words of wisdom have been thought to suggest some acquaintance with the teachings of the Apostle Paul, took advantage of the favor of his pupil and master, the Emperor Nero, to amass during four years of unique prosperity, no less a property than would be represented by fifteen million dollars. Having possessed himself of this immense fortune he proceeded, moralist and philosopher although he was, first to build his house and then to furnish it with objects of art of the most costly description.

The suggestion of Goethe is interesting and well sustained, that the Romans never went beyond the condition of *parvenus*, their luxury being nothing but "tasteless extravagance and vulgar ostentation." Even their architecture departed from the severe Grecian idea of beauty and contented itself with size and ornament, as appears in the Colosseum, Hadrian's Villa, and the Baths of Caracalla. They delighted in the bigness of their structures and in decorations of gold, silver and precious stones. In the appointments of private houses the spirit of rivalry drove each new emperor or affluent prince to further excess of ex-

The Moral Standards of the Period

penditure. For a while the palace of Lucullus was accounted the finest in Rome, but in a few years it was surpassed by hundreds of mansions which vied with each other in size and splendor. The process of enlargement and enrichment went on until the summit of extravagance was reached in the Golden House of Nero, with its decorations of incomparable magnificence, and its beautiful setting of parks, woods, pools and fountains. The colonades of the house itself were a Roman mile in length. Within were masterpieces of Greek art; while beneath a roof which rested on enormous columns were walls which glistened with gold and pearls. Not far below it in magnificence was the palace of Domitian which hinted of the magic touch which belongs to tales of fancy. Such lavish expenditure was not confined to emperors, nor to the capital, for it covered with parks and villas, the Campania, the Sabine Hills, even the lake shores of the north.

In dress and personal adornment the same passion for display ran to extremes. Pliny tells of a Roman lady arrayed for a betrothal feast, itself a hollow mockery, in a gown covered with pearls and emeralds, at a cost which would have fed and clothed every hungry and naked person in the populous city. Display became the talisman of success. Ju-

In The Time of Paul

venal declared that not even a Cicero could earn two pounds at the bar unless he wore a conspicuous gold ring; and that to succeed a man must be often seen borne through the crowded streets on a litter and making sumptuous purchases of rich vases and beautiful slaves; that he must also wear brilliant robes and flashing jewels, for only then could he demand fabulous prices for his services as a pleader.

This parade of riches continued to the tragic end, and literally attended a man to his tomb, leaving him only when he had visibly left the earth. Even at death there was an exhibition of ornaments belonging to the deceased, a procession of hired mourners, mutes who with dishevelled hair made a show of voiceless grief, beating their breasts in mockery of a sorrow which no one felt. Criers went about the streets to announce the death and the hour of the funeral. The procession passed through the most crowded quarters of the city and made itself noisy with varied demonstrations of simulated woe. If the deceased had been prominent in public affairs the cortege moved on to the Forum for the funeral oration, which fulsomely celebrated not only his own honors and glories but also those of his ancestors. The mourning train then passed without the

The Moral Standards of the Period

city walls and the grotesque ceremonies were concluded at a funeral pyre, where all the emblems of a vain show were consumed and the body reduced to the ashes which alone remained to typify the reality of a life so vainly passed and so lightly mourned.

With this morbid devotion to pleasure went an equally abnormal lack of humanity. While absorbed in the pursuit of immediate happiness men became not only indifferent to the misery of others but even found delight in their outcries of terror and pain. The gigantic system of slavery with which the state burdened itself brought with it in the acutest form a sense of the embarrassment of riches. Millions of slaves, without citizenship or manhood, without family or social ties, without self respect or self restraint, were a constant source of apprehension. Desperate deeds were always a possibility and an insurrection which would have arrayed the majority—wronged, furious, irresponsible—against property and life, was a ceaseless dread. Yet the utter lack of intelligent sympathy and humane consideration sustained in its worst form an institution monstrous in its denial of every human right and in the infliction of hopeless misery.

Callous to the anguish and despair of fellow creatures, whom the precepts of philosophers taught them to treat as chattels, Romans of the lordly class corrupted with public exhibition of torture and bloodshed not themselves only, but the populace whom they despised. Every fantastic device was resorted to for the excitement of jaded minds, every form of fierce and bloody contest was adopted to furnish entertainment for blasé spectators, men, women, and children. Such hardness of heart, such dullness of sensibility, almost passes belief, and yet contemporary literature abounds in tales which bring to modern minds unspeakable horror. The people not only learned to endure the sight of blood; they craved it. The menacing cry of the rabble which made Augustus and Trajan tremble on the throne of so vast an empire was, "Bread and Games!" Invention and resources were put to the stretch to meet this wolfish demand for blood It is recorded that a single emperor brought to Rome more than three thousand wild beasts, and forced into the amphitheatre no fewer than eight thousand gladiators. When the monotony of ordinary scenes of violence made them weary, all possible changes having been rung on the fight of criminals for life and gladiators for fame and money, of human beings with lions and tigers, and of stranger beasts with each other, they

The Moral Standards of the Period

turned to the ludicrous. A Roman mob must be amused at any cost of treasure or decency. Fierce, discordant cries passed into the wild laughter of buffoonery as men who were blindfolded rushed upon each other with the clumsy fury of desperation, followed by deformed and dwarfed creatures whose misshapen misery enhanced its tasteless pleasure. What mercy could live in such an atmosphere! What sensibilities could survive such sights and sounds! The entire populace was involved in the passion for bloodshed, the noblest and wisest uttering scarcely a word of protest, even Cicero venturing no further than to say: "Some consider the games cruel, and possibly they are as now conducted!"

Cruelty and lust have always been found in ill-omened conjunction, though it would be difficult to give a philosophical reason for their union. The men who lost the sense of pity gained correspondingly in the basest passions, so that the evils which dismayed observers of that age threatened the overthrow of the whole social structure. Lucian wrote with bitter sarcasm: "If any one loves wealth and power, if any one has wholly surrendered himself to pleasures, full tables, carousals and lewdness, let him go to Rome." The historian Levy declared, "Rome has become great by her virtues till now, when we can neither bear our vices nor their remedies." It was a shameless, debauched age, as the relics of indecency on the walls of Pompeii and Herculaneum report with unseemly accuracy. The majority of poets and wits, and every theatre of the day fed with their unspeakable obscenities an appetite for baseness which demanded the lowest and grossest forms of excitement. Even the virtuous and refined Pliny indulged in salacious epigrams. Martial and Statius, who are among the most brilliant representatives of the Flavian era, disfigured their writings with vile allusions. Nearly all plays were spiced with profanity and indelicacies, while sallies against the first principles of morality and jests at the expense of the gods made the theatres ring with coarse laughter. Baseness was in the very air poisoning and corrupting each new generation of youth.

This was a sad fall from the stern morality of early Rome. The Latins, in their integrity, held fast the sentiments of chastity and modesty, for hundreds of years a divorce being unheard of. The family was maintained with love and respect, marriage being held sacred and motherhood being regarded as the noblest estate conceivable. Even nude images of the gods were not tolerated. With Greek culture

The Moral Standards of the Period

came luxury and effeminacy until, as Uhlhorn has said, "the ancient simple domesticity disappeared and with it chastity and morality." The voluptuousness and groveling baseness of life at Rome make a record so dark and tragic that one gladly turns down such pages of history, hoping to shut out the dismal fact that a civilization, once so brilliant, could have fallen into such hopeless decay.

The reason for this widespread social corruption is ultimately to be found in the absence of any power that could make for righteousness. Men were left to fight evil without weapons, to maintain virtue without the inspiration of noble examples, or the encouragement of divine grace. The finer ideals and types of character were unknown. It has been said by a modern student of the times that Cato the elder possessed almost every virtue not specially commended of Christ, but that there was not one of the beatitudes in which he, the best of the Romans, could have claimed a part; and that there was not one of the divinities who possessed any virtue at all. Epictetus boasted that one who is wise "fears neither man nor God," and Seneca follows in the same strain, saying that "From man not much is to be feared; from God, nothing." The spirit of reverence did not belong to men who possessed

In The Time of Paul

neither a profound respect for virtue, nor an exalted sense of deity.

Christianity found only the ineradicable moral nature upon which to build a structure of personal character and social righteousness. This was apparently a slender base for the lordly edifice which belonged to the new scheme of life, but it was sufficient. Insincerity, as well as baseness, were rife; but the fact that men sometimes spoke in behalf of virtue, and that men encouraged such utterances, betokened a moral sense which at the worst was only dormant. It may be true of Seneca, as Macaulay wrote, that, "the business of a philosopher was to declaim in praise of poverty with two million sterling at usury, to meditate epigramatic conceits about the evils of luxury in gardens which moved the envy of sovereigns, to rant about liberty while fawning on the insolent and pampered freedman of a tyrant, to celebrate the divine beauty of virtue with a pen which had just before written a defence of the murder of a mother by her son." Nevertheless, the fine sentiments testified to the existence of a moral ideal and the possibility of real excellence of character, as was abundantly exhibited in such men as the slave-philosopher Epictetus, and the imperial philosopher Marcus Aurelius ; in the incorruptible Fabricius, the

The Moral Standards of the Period

high-minded Regulus, the industrious and frugal Cincinnatus; in Virgil, also a poet of delicate fancies; and in Cicero, an eloquent pleader for public virtue. There remained enough of moral understanding to make the task of an Apostle not altogether hopeless. The world not only needed a gospel of righteousness and assurances of divine grace, but it was prepared for a message of light given with the urgency of an ambassador of Christ. Therefore, Paul could write to one Roman colony: "Let your conversation be always with grace, seasoned with salt," that is, with the salt of refinement and delicacy, and to another colony, "Whatsoever things are true, whatsoever things are honorable, whatsoever things are just, whatsoever things are pure, whatsoever things are lovely, whatsoever things are of good report; if there be any virtue, and if there be any praise, take account of these things."

CHAPTER VII.

THE INTELLECTUAL TENDENCIES OF THE TIME.

AGAINST the dark background of social corruption and the frightful debasement of the enslaved and beggared masses gleams the light of intelligence. The mind had found quickening and expansion. By the intellectual development of the age of Pericles and Augustus the way had been prepared for the story and even for the philosophy of Christianity. The Word was not proclaimed to dull and groveling savages, wanting in language and mental capacity, but had free course to run and be glorified in the most perfect speech of history. The significance of this fact has been demonstrated in our own century by the slowness of mission work among barbarous people. It required thirty years of devout labor to produce the first convert among the savage tribes of West Africa; but now, in the developed science of the third generation of missionaries, the school and the college keep pace with the advancing tide of evangelistic work. Ignorance is not the mother of that kind of devotion upon which Christianity is built. The appeal of Christianity is to reason, through the medium of human speech, and its doctrines require the finest and noblest modes of expression. No literature is loftier, no lines of reasoning more subtle than those given to the world from the exalted mind of Saint Paul.

The perfection of the Greek language, which he employed in his letters to the churches, and in which he preached as his native tongue, has been conceded by scholars of all lands and ages. It was naturally, and yet providentially, developed by a people who for pure intellectuality have never been surpassed. It is at once the richest and most exact, the most flexible and the most delicate the world has yet known. Its vocabulary is extensive while its grammatical structure admits of the most varied and refined methods of expression. Like the art and architecture of Greece it was not only a part of the evolution of a unique people, but it served to perpetuate and transmit the intellectuality out of which it had been developed. The language contained much more than can be attributed to the independent out-working of Grecian genius. No people has ever been entirely isolated.

In The Time of Paul

There has never been a hermit nation. At least no race has lifted itself out of savagery save as it absorbed ideas and inherited institutions from other sources of civilization. Even the Hittites, shut away from contemporary kingdoms beyond the Taurus and Phrygian ranges, came down to Hamal and touched the headwaters of the Euphrates at Carchemish, thus acquiring knowledge from the Egyptians and the Assyrians, which, in turn, they contributed to people with whom they established commercial relations across the Hellespont. The continuity of history has never been more clearly exhibited than in the structure of civilization which made the Augustan age memorable.

The language and art of Greece was Rome's by right of inheritance, a right fortified by independent and vigorous effort to improve what had been discovered and absorbed. The civilization of Rome was still more complex and derivative because the Empire had swept its boundaries around all the lands which had been directly and indirectly influenced by Greek culture, assimilating whatever was fitted to advance society and enrich the state. The elements which entered into the composite order of the first century were exceedingly ancient. Not all of them can be traced to

Intellectual Tendencies of the Time

their origin, as not every great river can be followed to its source among the wooded hills. The streams of influence which flowed together at last in the common life of the great empire took their rise among the Babylonians, Egyptians and Phœnicians. From one source came the love of magnificence, from another the sense of grandeur, from another suggestions as wide apart as commerce and literature. The process began in prehistoric times, but its beginnings are forever lost; the accumulative effects, however, lingered to Paul's day, and vitally affected the fortunes of Christianity. The Romans had varied culture because they learned from the Greeks, while the Greeks had become the masters of the world in literature, art and philosophy, because they had gathered treasures of thought and experience from so many lands.

It was not only a time of vast accumulations, but also of intellectual activity. It is true that the greatest thinkers had long passed away. The unsurpassed triad of original and progressive philosophers, Socrates, Plato and Aristotle, coming in succession as master and pupil, had lived their fruitful lives and gone to the shades. Homer, the first and greatest of epic writers; Æschylus, Sophocles, and Euripides, masters of Greek tragedy, and Herod-

In The Time of Paul

otus, the father of all historians, had long before completed their tasks; but Latin writers of the first century found their inspiration in the Greek classics. Athens, in the time of the Empire, bore the character of a university town to which every Roman of literary pretensions made a pilgrimage. Cicero delighted in its atmosphere of culture. Hadrian was proud to have embellished it with imperial magnificence. This was an age of travel, brigandage and piracy having been suppressed by the fleets and armies of the Empire. Men who boasted the rights of Roman citizenship went everywhere in safety. All who had leisure and money betook themselves to classic and historic scenes, quickening and broadening their minds by the easy and swift adoption of whatever they discovered in the kindred civilization of the people whom Rome had conquered in the contest of arms, but to whom she yielded the palm of victory in the contest of ideas. Latins and Greeks were of the same Aryan stock, and although each branch of the common race had developed under different environments, yet the likeness was deeper than the divergence. Therefore the moment they came into contact assimilation was measurably complete. Out of this communication of ideas came a new and worthy

Intellectual Tendencies of the Time

literature. To this century belonged such poets as Horace, Virgil and Ovid, such satirists as Juvenal and Lucian, such historians as Sallust, Tacitus and Plutarch, such philosophers as Seneca and Epictetus. It was the golden age of the Latins, and even emperors became patrons of letters and the arts.

Greco-Roman civilization was no longer confined to the two historic peninsulas. It had followed the conquests of the phalanx and the legion until it had touched all centers of life in the known world. Cicero, who was governor of Cilicia fifty years before the time of Paul, speaks of the thorough acquaintance with Greek among all literary classes. About the close of the Apostle's career, Agricola, who was to become conqueror of Britain, was receiving a Greek education in the city of Marseilles. In Pamphylia and Galatia there were many cities which had been so far Hellenized that the gospel could be proclaimed in them through the language which had become the vehicle of revelation.

The introduction of social and educational influences was Rome's most effective way of subduing rustic barbarism and overcoming oriental stagnation. This policy originated with the great Macedonian whose ambition had first carried the language of Greece into the Orient, and of the Greek kings of Syria who, in the breaking up of the Alexandrian empire, served in turn to spread and deepen the new civilization. The special work of the first century was the furtherance of an undertaking which had been shared in by many generations; and which at first had moved from Macedonia eastward, and which afterward moved from Italy in other directions. In many cities far from Rome were not only examples and reproductions of Grecian art, but schools and libraries open to the public. Pliny was delighted to learn that copies of his works were sold in Lyons, while along the banks of the Danube and Rhine were manufactories of earthenware of the Hellenic type. Everywhere men were being educated in ancient and current literature; in art and philosophy, in history and social science, in agriculture and war.

This widespread intelligence not only opened the way for an apprehension of the Gospel but it in turn reacted upon Christianity itself, which was seeking to enlighten the world. No new disclosures were made and no revision of the apostolic message was attempted, but independence in interpreting and applying it was inevitable; with a certain molding and remolding of the institutions of Christianity. The processes of religious development have

Intellectual Tendencies of the Time

always followed their own law. Christianity has, therefore, been compelled to adjust itself, for the time being to established ways of thinking. This was specially true in the first century when its doctrines were acted upon by currents of thought and feeling older than itself and almost as persistent, and when its noblest precepts were being insensibly modified by public sentiment. The unfolding of a seed depends in part upon the peculiar quality of the soil into which it happens to fall. The seed of the Word has had variant fortunes in the different soils in which it has been planted. The hereditary tendencies of the Roman world exerted such an influence upon the life and the mold of Christianity that after nineteen centuries they still shape and control it.

After a time men learned to philosophize about religion and to add the sanction of reason to that of revelation and command; but there was nothing of this in the ancient religions, for not one of them addressed itself in a formal and undisguised way to reason. The Grecian and Roman mythologies were childish and their sacred rites superstitious, while the Hebrew prophets rested upon the authority of a divine mandate. It did not belong to the Semitic habit of mind to rationalize. A certain limitation was put upon the Founder of

In The Time of Paul

Christianity, who could deal with men only as He found them. The language of Greece would not have been altogether strange to many of His hearers, but the language of philosophy would have been puzzling, and distracting. The men of Judea had not learned to love knowledge for its own sake, nor had they become adepts in following processes by which truth is established in the mind. They were not much concerned about the principle of things. They had never been taught to assign rational cases for natural phenomena, or rational grounds for moral precepts. They were interested in neither the process nor the product of ratiocination. They simply listened favorably to that which bore the marks of authority or which commended itself immediately to their minds.

There is profound philosophy in the Sermon on the Mount, but there is no formal philosophizing in any of the New Testament deliverances. It was left for another people to bring in this habit of mind and to arrive by another pathway at the conclusions which had been authoritatively announced by Christ and His apostles. No road has been discovered leading to sublimer heights than those on which the Master always dwelt, but another approach has been discovered by which to

Intellectual Tendencies of the Time

measure their loftiness and to appreciate the outlook from their summit. The services of the synagogue, the schools of the rabbis, even the teachings of the apostles, had failed to develop certain intellectual faculties which the finer and broader culture of Greece brought into play. With this disciplined thought men could go to the foundation of ethical systems, could discover the right and the significance of man's relations to nature and God, and then set forth more clearly and persuasively the ideal ends and aims of human life.

Under the stimulus and instruction of Greek philosophers, men who had received the word of revelation learned to apply reason to the existence of the soul. Thus they deepened their sense of spiritual realities and intensified their longings for the heavenly life. The authoritative utterance of revelation sufficed for a people not given to speculation and reflection, but there was unmeasured gain in the freedom from the dogmatism concerning himself. The soul asserts itself to unspeakable advantage in conscience and consciousness. The authenticity of a document may be questioned. The prerogative of command may be denied, but the independent, autocratic dictum of the mind concerning its own modes and laws of existence cannot be rejected. It was, therefore, no small contribution of Greek thought that established two moral existences in the universe, God the Creator, and man created in his moral likeness.

It is not to be conceded that the rational process was complete apart from the authority and guidance of revelation. The loftiest of philosophers fell short of the New Testament standard of thought regarding the capacity and destiny of man, but they traced the way to absolute convictions concerning the immaterial nature of the soul in contrast with the crass and perishable nature of the body. Socrates was the pioneer in this splendid field of research. He was fascinated by the mysteries and grandeurs revealed within. His favorite injunction to his pupils was, "Know thyself," an injunction which he was the first to obey. The fact of the soul and its possible moral improvement were the objects of his unfailing interest and speculation. To him all material considerations were unpractical. Man and whatever relates to man furnished the only matters worthy of deep study. Plato had the immense advantage of such a forerunner, and also of the possession of a more thoroughly disciplined mind, and consequently he came to a profounder knowledge of the soul. He made much of the principle of intelligence, by virtue of which man has kinship with God, and hence is superior to all other forms of creation.

Connected with this demonstration of the soul was the closely allied one which resulted in convictions concerning God. Which of these two antedated the other and which was of greater value cannot be easily determined. Contributions were made by successive generations of "seekers after God" until at last the idea of God was confidently grasped. Out of the varied forms and modes of being these truth seekers unraveled the enigma presented in the apparent contradictions of nature by the clearly asserted principle of unity of purpose. They brought "the phenomena of earth and sea and sky under a single expression." By the "unconscious alchemy of thought" the separate groups of phenomena were combined into a whole and conceived of as forming a "universe." The search was continued until the force which pervades the universe was reached. There can be but one God, and to Him, by further elaboration of thought, they were compelled to attribute mind and personality, together with the prerogatives of moral government. In ordering the vast whole of nature

In The Time of Paul

according to immutable law He must be supreme.

Having no resources of knowledge save unaided reason, their doctrine of Deity was neither complete nor free from error. Socrates did not deny the existence and activity of gods, many, while maintaining that there is one Supreme Being to whom reverence must ever be paid. His arguments, like those of the Christian Paley, move irresistibly toward a Designer of the universe. Both reasoned from the amazing structure of the body whose various parts play into each other for a common end; both dwelling with special delight on the marvelous organ of vision. To indications of purpose drawn from various adaptations in nature, such as birds to the air and fish to the sea, he added others which apply to the life within. He was wont to ask: "Are you not conscious of reason and intelligence? And yet do you doubt intelligence elsewhere in the great universe! You believe in the unseen soul, and do you yet refuse to believe in the unseen God?"

Here again, the profounder mind of Plato, building upon the originality and moral earnestness of his master, advanced to yet higher ideas of God as the "Father and Maker of the universe." To him the doctrine of atheism was such an absurdity that he considered it possible only to "lost and perverted natures," and hence be justified the moral indignation of those who had come to a normal belief in Deity. Like Socrates he fell into the obstinate error of the time and marred his theism with the inconsistent notion of subordinate gods who create in obedience to the mandate of the great Designer; but he advanced, nevertheless, to ideas of God's providental care over men, which wrought good results even out of poverty, sickness, and misfortune.

Such notions of God lacked authority and fullness but they prepared men's minds for the revelations of the Gospel, and so leavened the thought of the world as to make a rational theism and a living faith more easily attained and more firmly held.

As Greek philosophy applied reason to God and the soul, so also did it elucidate the grounds of ethical obligation. It raised morals to the rank of a science; but not in the sense that it made duty more sublime or that it added aught to the treasures of the Sermon on the Mount. The system of ethics introduced by the teaching and enforced by the example of Christ was not susceptible of improvement. But there was an advantage in looking at the same truth from a new viewpoint, and in approaching it with a new mental furnishing.

For the first time, in any land, men were given to moralizing, to reasoning out the grounds of right, and defining the relations of man to nature and God. To this had been applied the deepest thinking of the Hellenic world, for "philosophy was absorbed by ethics." Plato was profoundly concerned with this aspect of the truth that man bears the image of divine intelligence. He declared that each one has two patterns before him, the one blessed and divine, the other godless and wretched. From the manifested character of God he reasoned as to the nature and scope of virtue. "God is altogether righteous, to become like him is to become holy, just, and wise." He lacked, however, the appreciation of love, and missed the virtue of pity; and not knowing the doctrine of grace he limited his promises of refinement to philosophers; easily excluding, as did his great pupil, Aristotle, the unfortunate masses; and yet he pressed on toward the goal of righteousness.

Moral questions gave impulse also to the Stoic system of philosophy, which from the first took a practical turn, seeking to discover the actual laws of life and to bring men into harmony with their environment. In its earlier stages it blundered, keeping too close to materialism, yet maintaining a certain directness of aim which interested and moved men. The veriest child of gospel training could have helped such philosophers out of many of their difficulties; and yet they were grandly striving to discover the secret of virtue and the inner principle of light. At their highest point they fell far short of perfection and altogether missed the fact of God's graciousness, yet they established lines of investigation which could be afterward followed under the light of Christianity.

To both Jew and Christian the idea of right was identified with holy laws. To the Greek mind "divine commands" were not an arbitrary expression of a personal will, but rather of nature, of laws which belonged to the very constitution of the universe. It was the part of man to employ the powers and faculties with which he had been endowed for the apprehension of these laws and for the proper adjustment to them of all his activities. As he constructed a rational idea of the Creator and Moral Governor of the world, so he was bound to discover the ethical relationship of man. It was evident that the universe was fashioned for wise and beneficent ends, for the production of beauty and happiness. What,

In The Time of Paul

then, is the meaning of the countless miseries of mankind? How can these things be fitted to an ever deepening belief in divine goodness? Men must be the authors of their own misery. They must have wilfully failed to seek conformity with the harmonious laws of nature. The responsibility for the jarring discord is with intelligent and free beings.

This idea was not born in maturity. It is too fundamental and far-reaching to have come at once to perfection and dominance. Two facts were first established, and then the relation between them was formulated. These two facts are that man thinks and acts. But action must depend upon the "assent of the mind;" for mere impulse toward an object does not justify possession. There must, therefore, be an exercise of judgment on the basis of the laws of nature, then the will comes into play, and ought always to accord with the highest good of the whole being. The modern philosopher expresses no more than this when he declares that man has self-determining power and that he is under everlasting obligation to bring himself into harmony with his proper environment.

This idea of fixedness in nature and freedom in man found forcible utterance in the writings of Epictetus. "Of all things that are, one

Intellectual Tendencies of the Time

part is in our control and the other out of it. Out of our control are our bodies, property, reputation and office; in our control are opinion, impulse to do, effort to obtain and to avoid; in a word, our own proper activities." He maintained, with his fellow-Stoics, that it not only belongs to man to educate his mind and train his will, but that it is the province of nature to advance the process of discipline. In this way the Stoics justified the wisdom and goodness of God and encouraged man to the highest exercise of virtue. The Christian philosophers of Alexandria took up this suggestion with delight, and enriched it with precepts from the Gospels, until they had evolved an elaborate doctrine of God as "the Teacher, Trainer, and Physician of men." The heathen philosophers led the way to the inspiring thought that man needs only to gain the prize which has been put within his reach. Thus he acquires finest qualities of soul, putting passion under control of reason, and living in accord with the beneficent will of God. The path which these thinkers followed brought them to sincerity, which lies, indeed, near the foundations of Christian character. They did not touch such of the Beatitudes as "Blessed are the poor in spirit;" "Blessed are the meek;" "Blessed are the merciful;" "Blessed are those who hunger for righteousness;" but they caught glimpses of that principle of goodness which had been overlooked by the formalists of the temple. They discovered the ethical quality of secret thoughts and cherished impulses.

Epictetus held that the philosopher's lecture room should be a surgery, where men should not be entertained by fair words, but where they should be aided in the dissection of their own characters, in the detection of secret faults which could be banished from the soul. He followed out a principle which had been recognized from the first by the Stoics, who laid emphasis upon the inwardness of man's real life, and he unfailingly insisted that motive counts for more than performance. In the time of greatest glory for this system of philosophy, Epictetus, Seneca and Aurelius urged strict examination of one's own character, even to minute inspection of words and deeds which marked each day of life.

The chief advantage of such habits of observation and reflection was not that Grecian standards approached those of Christianity, for all the philosophy of the first century was impotent against the social corruption of the age, but that the new religion found many minds

Intellectual Tendencies of the Time

prepared for its sweet and holy revelations, and that it secured a worthy handmaid in the reason which had already been trained to noble uses. The Greeks, as well as the Hebrews, proved themselves "a people of God's own possession," set apart to the highest service of God and man. In a qualified way, the Stoic, as well as the prophet, was a forerunner of the Christ; nay, like the Apostle also, he came after the gospel to expound and apply its revelations and injunctions. While not many "wise," while not many who are exalted in the conceit of their own knowledge are called, yet the appeal of Christianity is always to an understanding mind, in behalf of an intelligent faith.

We gratefully recognize, therefore, the glorious mission of these two kindred peoples, the Greeks and the Latins, to quicken the human intellect, to cultivate the imagination, to refine the taste, and even to discover the rational grounds of faith and character. As the Renaissance ushered in a new day for vital religion, so in the first century the splendid development of the human faculties made possible the phenomenally rapid spread of Christianity throughout the vast empire of Rome. Beyond the bounds of civilization it did not attempt to go. Elsewhere in the barbaric

In The Time of Paul

world, the seed would have fallen on unproductive ground. Under the ægis of Rome the greatest herald of the cross found protection, and by a light which shined out of Athens he led men to the truth which had first been proclaimed in Jerusalem.

CHAPTER VIII.

The Inevitable Conflict and Victory.

THERE have been many crises in the world's history, but it is hardly correct to say that in all of them an issue of supreme moment was involved. At the battle of Marathon the Persian host was turned back from ruthlessly despoiling Achaia and destroying the civilization of Greece. Now it would doubtless have been an incalculable loss to the world to have had the progressive life of Athens checked or perhaps even extinguished by Oriental despotism—art, philosophy, civil government having been wrought into forms of perfection by the genius of the most enterprising and original people of ancient times; yet it would be an hyperbole to say that the hope of mankind was staked upon the result of an attack made by the Grecian phalanx which on the third day of the Persian invasion dared to beat against the dense mass of Xerxes' army. The world was not saved by Grecian arms, nor has it been saved by Grecian culture.

In The Time of Paul

On the banks of the Metaurus an army under the Consul Nero struck with fury the camp of the Carthagenians, and by noontime had won a victory of lasting renown. For seventeen years Hanibal had maintained himself in Italy, ravaging it at will from the snowy Alps to the Straits of Messina, and only waited that fateful spring for the arrival of the allied forces which his brother had led through Spain and Southern Gaul, to appear before the gates of Rome. It would be difficult to estimate the loss which would have resulted to the world from the substitution of that hard, cruel, materialistic, uncommunicative type of civilization which had been wrought in North Africa, for the radically different type which was being developed on the Sabine hills; a civilization not only independent and vigorous, but destined to enlarge itself by the absorption of all that was being evolved by the kindred race in the Grecian peninsula. Yet it would be extravagant to say that the life of the world was at issue when in the grey light of the morning Hasdrubal's army was routed in a desperate encounter that rescued Rome from threatened annihilation. The victory was important, but not absolutely vital to the interests of mankind.

There have been crises in the history of

The Inevitable Conflict and Victory

Christianity when much (but not all) was at stake. When Abdurman crossed the Pyrenees with a countless horde of followers, fierce and ruthless, and after ravaging Southern France met Charles Martel near Poitiers in mortal combat, Mohammedanism threatened to supplant Christianity in Central Europe. The consequences of such a victory as the Moorish chief counted on with easy assurance would have been direful in the extreme, but one would not be warranted in declaring it a fatal blow to the cause of Christian civilization. It might have delayed the march of events, but not the final development of freedom, intelligence and pure religion.

If Luther had yielded at the Diet of Worms, as a weaker man might have done, under the combined threats of the hierarchy and the officials of state, the Reformation would have waited a century, and that movement of the world toward better things which resulted from the co-ordinate advance of commerce, the revival of learning, the discovery of printing and the rejuvenation of the church, would have lacked its most essential feature. No one who has in mind the significance of the outcome can read the story of Luther's critical hour save with bated breath; and yet there is no ground for saying that the cause of pure religion had come to its ultimate contest. Christianity might be over-run in particular lands, as it was by Islamism in Asia Minor and Egypt in the eighth century, or banished from a country where promising missions were established as in China in a later century, and yet maintain such a vigorous a hold elsewhere as to insure its continuance on the earth.

But the result of the fight which the Apostle Paul was making against the allied forces of the Empire was absolute and final. It closely resembled the issue of his Master's work in the narrower field of Palestine. If the Messiah had failed to develop in some minds the truth of His message, the glory of His personality, the spiritual power of His kingdom, His coming would have been in vain. If Paul had failed, in a ministry much longer and more extended than his Master's, to build some enduring churches out of Gentile material, the defeat would have carried with it appalling consequences. He was fully accredited as an ambassador of Christ; he had the tongue of fire in which to proclaim his divine message; as a Hebrew he could enter the synagogues; and as a Roman he had the freedom of every city of the Empire. If he had not been able to quicken faith, arouse devotion, inspire hope, against a heathen philosphy, a dominant re-

The Inevitable Conflict and Victory

ligion and a tide of worldliness, then no man could take up the enterprise which had failed in his hands. The divine attempt to plant spiritual righteousness and a holy faith would have come to abysmal disaster. The utmost had been done in heaven and on earth. No other experiment could hope for success. There remained no further sacrifice for sin, no sweeter expression of mercy and grace, no more pathetic and persuasive appeal to a lost world. Against the heaviest odds the Apostle must win. The issue was absolutely vital. Here was the crisis which involves the life of mankind, the veritable redemption of the world.

When the effort of Paul was crowned with success the victory was not for himself alone but mainly for the cause to which he had devoted his life. The day was won for Christianity. It had been demonstrated that it could gain and hold the ground against the allied forces of the heathen world, against superstition, against a self-sufficient philosophy, against evil customs and rampant passions, against malignant and persistent prosecution. Men and women were to be found in every province of the Empire who followed the example of devotion set by the Apostle, suffering stripes and imprisonment and ofttimes facing, death for the faith of the Gospel. Better still,

In The Time of Paul

a new type of individual and social life had been produced. Out of the formalities of Judaism and the grossness of heathenism had been gathered many people whom Paul could address as "brethren," "faithful followers," and even "saints in the Lord." Before he began his ministry at Rome he was assured that the Capital contained some who were "beloved of God." From Asia Minor he wrote elaborate letters to "the Church of God" which had been gathered under his prolonged ministry at Corinth—a most worldly and self-absorbed city, containing, nevertheless, a few whom he personally knew to be "sanctified in Christ Jesus," and to be in loving fellowship with other "saints" scattered through "the whole of Achaia." Even in Ephesus, where the passion for gladiatorial games fell little short of that which demoralized the populace of Rome, and where the temples were crowded by the superstitious worshipers of Diana, there was a reliable company of saints who were "faithful in Christ Jesus," and who were so thoughtful and intelligent that the Apostle could send them a treatise only once surpassed in profundity of Christian doctrine. In Macedonia there were two churches of such noble faith that Paul was grateful beyonds words for every message that reached him concerning

The Inevitable Conflict and Victory

their development in the grace of the Gospel. One was at Thessalonica, from which city he had been driven by an infuriated mob; where men "turned from their idols to serve a living and true God," suffering "much affliction" because of the "joy of the Holy Ghost," until the report of their faith "to God-ward" filled even neighboring provinces. The other church was at Philippi, the city to which he had first come after crossing the Ægean Sea, and to which he sent the most affectionate and glowing of all his epistles.

There was no shadow of doubt in the mind of the Apostle concerning the ultimate success of the Gospel. When his own labors were drawing to an end he wrote to younger men who had been consecrated to office in the administration of the church, warning them, indeed, against heresies and worldly tendencies; yet speaking with unshaken confidence of the final triumph of Him, who had brought life and immortality to light. In fact, he looked for a speedy development of the divine plans in the glorious coming of the Lord, building his exultant expectations, doubtless, upon the astounding achievements of truth and grace which his own eyes had witnessed. No human mind can so explore the future as to read the details of unwritten history. Divine illumination and wide experience gave the Apostle blessed assurance that the power and wisdom of God, as manifested in Christ, were sufficient for the redemption of the world, but it was as impossible as it was unnecessary for him to know how long and complex is the process of evolution for the Kingdom of God on earth.

By the end of the first century the seed of truth had been planted in many lands, in fields which were to be swept by storms, and crossed and re-crossed by contending armies. The Empire was to be over-run by barbarians and finally dismembered. New nations and new types of civilization were to arise. The old order of things was to be overturned. New modes of government, new systems of education, new lines of social structure, new and divisive methods of thought and worship in the church were to succeed each other through successive centuries. Through all these changes the Gospel which Paul preached was to maintain itself with unabated power and unmodified grace. As in the first century, it sustained itself against ideas, habits, customs and institutions which had not only to be resisted but actually transformed. The "prince of this world" does not readily yield to the powers of light. Selfishness and worldliness are entrenched in the perversions of human

The Inevitable Conflict and Victory

nature. Consequently Christianity can not lay down the task assumed when its Founder came to earth until the last traces of untruth and unkindliness have yielded to the persuasions of heavenly grace.

But the day dawned. The light deepened in the eastern skies. Its radiance gladdened the eyes of men who in the time of Paul were gathering courage from the earliest victories of the Word. Each critical age has added its triumphs to the list of glories, and each succeeding generation has had larger assurance than its predecessor that the time must come when all the kingdoms which men have claimed as their own, shall belong to Him whose right it is to rule, and be but provinces of the world-wide Empire of the Living God.